Vue.js for Beginners: Build Dynamic and Responsive Web Apps

A Step-by-Step Guide to Mastering Front-End Development with Vue.js

BOOZMAN RICHARD

BOOKER BLUNT

Table of Content

TABLE OF CONTENTS

INTRODUCTION 6

Why Vue.js? 6

What Will You Learn in This Book? 7

Why This Book? 9

Who Should Read This Book? 11

How is This Book Structured? 11

Conclusion 12

Chapter 1 14

Introduction to Vue.js 14

    Summary: 21

Chapter 2 22

Vue.js Basics 22

    Summary: 30

Chapter 3 32

The Vue Lifecycle 32

    Summary: 42

Chapter 4 43

Vue Components: The Building Blocks 43

    Summary: 55

Chapter 5 56

Working with Vue Directives 56

Chapter 6 67

Data Binding in Vue 67

Chapter 7..80

Event Handling in Vue.js...80

Chapter 8..90

Computed Properties and Watchers.....................................90

Chapter 9..102

Vue Router: Adding Navigation to Your App.........................102

Chapter 10..115

State Management with Vuex..115

Chapter 11..128

Forms and Validation in Vue...128

Chapter 12..142

Working with APIs in Vue.js..142

Chapter 13..153

Vue.js Transitions and Animations......................................153

Chapter 14..164

Testing Vue.js Applications..164

Chapter 15..178

Best Practices for Vue.js Development................................178

Chapter 16..193

Building a Real-World Vue.js Application: Part 1..................193

Chapter 17..206

Building a Real-World Vue.js Application: Part 2..................206

Chapter 18..217

Building a Real-World Vue.js Application: Part 3..................217

Chapter 19..230

Vue.js and Responsive Web Design....................................230

Chapter 20..244

Handling User Authentication in Vue.js 244

Chapter 21 257

Deploying Vue.js Applications 257

Chapter 22 267

Vue.js Performance Optimization 267

Chapter 23 281

Security in Vue.js Applications 281

Chapter 24 295

Vue.js and Real-Time Applications 295

Chapter 25 308

Server-Side Rendering with Vue.js 308

Chapter 26 319

Vue 3 and the Composition API 319

Chapter 27 334

Advanced Topics in Vue.js 334

INTRODUCTION

In today's fast-paced world of web development, creating high-performance, scalable, and maintainable applications is crucial. Vue.js has become one of the most popular JavaScript frameworks due to its flexibility, simplicity, and powerful features that allow developers to create dynamic and interactive web applications. This book, **"Mastering Vue.js: A Comprehensive Guide to Building Scalable Web Applications,"** is designed to guide you through every aspect of Vue.js, from its basic building blocks to advanced concepts that will help you become an expert in creating Vue.js applications.

Whether you're a beginner looking to learn the fundamentals of Vue.js or an experienced developer seeking to deepen your understanding, this book offers a comprehensive, hands-on approach to mastering Vue.js. It provides a solid foundation for building web applications, incorporating both simple and complex features, with a particular focus on real-world scenarios and best practices.

Why Vue.js?

Vue.js stands out among other JavaScript frameworks due to its versatility. It can be used to create anything from simple single-page applications (SPAs) to complex, enterprise-level solutions. Vue's **reactivity system** enables real-time updates to the user interface, while its **component-based architecture** helps in creating reusable, modular code. The **Vue CLI** streamlines the process of setting up and managing projects, and the **Vue Router** and **Vuex** make routing and state management easier than ever.

Vue.js has grown into a modern front-end framework with a thriving ecosystem that provides solutions to common web development challenges. However, mastering Vue.js involves understanding how it integrates with a variety of other technologies, from server-side rendering (SSR) to real-time data updates. This book covers the entire breadth of Vue.js development, equipping you with the knowledge to create high-performing, scalable applications.

What Will You Learn in This Book?

This book is structured to guide you through both basic and advanced Vue.js concepts. As you progress through the chapters, you'll gain a deep understanding of the Vue.js ecosystem and its core concepts, including:

1. **Getting Started with Vue.js:**

o A solid introduction to Vue's foundational concepts such as the **Vue Instance**, **Directives**, **Data Binding**, and **Vue Components**.

o Setting up a Vue development environment and understanding the basic structure of a Vue app.

2. **Intermediate Concepts**:

o Exploring **Vue Router** to build multi-page applications.

o Handling state management with **Vuex**, especially in larger apps.

o Understanding the **Vue Lifecycle Hooks** and their use in managing component behavior.

3. **Advanced Topics**:

o Harnessing the power of the **Composition API** in Vue 3 for better organization of component logic and improved reusability.

o Utilizing **Server-Side Rendering (SSR)** for SEO-friendly web apps that load faster and are more performant.

o Handling **real-time updates** using WebSockets and libraries like **Socket.io** to build real-time applications.

4. **Vue.js in Practice**:

   o Refactoring legacy **Vue 2** codebases into Vue 3, adopting the **Composition API** for better maintainability.

   o Integrating **TypeScript** with Vue.js for better type safety and better development experiences.

   o Advanced patterns in **state management** and **mixins**, and building scalable applications with the right architecture.

5. **Real-World Examples**:

   o Throughout the book, you will work on real-world projects such as building a **real-time chat application**, a **complex dashboard**, and even a **Vue-based blog** with server-side rendering (SSR). These hands-on examples will help you apply what you've learned and build sophisticated, production-ready applications.

Why This Book?

- **Comprehensive Approach**: This book covers Vue.js from its most basic to its most advanced topics. We start with the fundamentals, giving you a solid foundation, and then build on that knowledge with advanced features and techniques.

- **Real-World Scenarios**: You won't just learn theory here. You will apply the concepts to real-world applications. Whether it's **Vue Router**, **Vuex**, or **SSR**, every chapter includes practical examples to reinforce your learning.

- **Vue 3**: As Vue 3 has brought powerful new features, including the **Composition API**, this book focuses on Vue 3 and helps you navigate its new capabilities for improved performance and developer experience.

- **Best Practices**: From **security** to **performance optimization** to **testing**, this book ensures that you are following best practices when building Vue.js applications, so you're not just learning how to use Vue but how to use it the right way.

- **Scalable Applications**: Building scalable, maintainable applications is essential as your projects grow. This book teaches you the principles of component-based architecture, modularity, and effective state management with **Vuex**, helping you build robust applications that are easy to maintain and extend.

Who Should Read This Book?

- **Beginners**: If you are new to Vue.js or front-end development, this book will introduce you to the world of Vue.js with a hands-on approach. You will gain a strong understanding of Vue's core concepts, including components, directives, and reactivity.
- **Intermediate Developers**: If you're already familiar with Vue.js, this book will deepen your knowledge by introducing you to advanced topics such as **Vuex, Vue Router, server-side rendering**, and **real-time applications**.
- **Experienced Vue Developers**: If you're an expert with Vue.js, this book offers a thorough exploration of new Vue 3 features like the **Composition API** and advanced patterns in **state management**, along with strategies to optimize performance and security in your applications.

How is This Book Structured?

Each chapter is designed to be both informative and practical. You'll learn new concepts, see them applied in examples, and then work on real-world projects that tie everything together.

- **Chapters 1-5**: Focus on the core concepts of Vue.js, from data binding and components to Vuex and Vue Router.

- **Chapters 6-10**: Delve into more advanced topics, including lifecycle hooks, custom directives, and performance optimization.

- **Chapters 11-15**: Cover the transition to Vue 3, server-side rendering, real-time applications, and modern tooling.

- **Chapters 16-20**: Focus on security, testing, and best practices for building scalable Vue.js applications.

- **Chapters 21-26**: Feature hands-on projects, including a blog, chat app, and complex dashboard app, demonstrating the application of advanced concepts and the best practices discussed in the book.

Conclusion

Whether you're just starting out with Vue.js or you're already a seasoned developer, **"Mastering Vue.js"** provides you with the tools, techniques, and knowledge to take your Vue development skills to the next level. By the end of this book, you'll not only be proficient in Vue.js but also have the practical experience needed to build and deploy modern, scalable web applications. Ready to start mastering Vue.js? Let's dive in!

CHAPTER 1

INTRODUCTION TO VUE.JS

What is Vue.js?

Vue.js is an open-source JavaScript framework used for building dynamic and interactive user interfaces, especially for single-page applications (SPAs). Created by Evan You in 2014, Vue.js is designed to be simple, flexible, and progressive, allowing developers to incrementally adopt its features without having to rewrite entire applications. Its core library focuses on the **view layer** (UI), which makes it easy to integrate with other libraries or existing projects.

Vue.js uses a declarative rendering system, meaning that developers only need to describe what the UI should look like based on the current state of the application. This approach helps create intuitive and efficient apps. Additionally, Vue's **reactive data binding** makes it easier to synchronize the UI with underlying data, simplifying development and improving performance.

In simple terms, Vue.js is a framework that helps you build applications that are easy to maintain, fast to develop, and provide great user experiences.

Why Choose Vue.js for Front-End Development?

Choosing Vue.js for front-end development offers several compelling advantages:

1. **Easy to Learn and Use**: Vue.js has a gentle learning curve compared to other front-end frameworks like Angular or React. Its syntax is simple and clear, which makes it an excellent choice for beginners.
2. **Lightweight**: Vue.js is incredibly lightweight, with its core library being only around 20KB in size. This ensures that your application will load faster and perform better.
3. **Flexibility and Integration**: Vue.js is highly flexible and can be integrated into any project without hassle. Whether you're building a complex single-page application (SPA) or enhancing an existing page, Vue.js fits easily into your workflow.
4. **Reactive Data Binding**: Vue.js automatically updates the view whenever data changes, reducing the need for manual DOM manipulation. This reactivity makes it efficient and productive for developers.
5. **Two-Way Data Binding**: Vue.js offers two-way data binding, meaning that changes in the UI can update the data model and vice versa. This is especially helpful for handling user input and form data.
6. **Comprehensive Ecosystem**: Vue's ecosystem includes various official tools, such as Vue Router (for routing),

Vuex (for state management), and Vue CLI (for project scaffolding). These tools simplify common development tasks and help developers build scalable applications.

7. **Community and Support**: Vue.js has a thriving community with an abundance of resources like tutorials, forums, and plugins. It also enjoys robust support from its core team and contributors.

8. **Performance**: Vue.js offers high performance and can handle complex applications efficiently. Its virtual DOM and optimized rendering system make it faster than traditional JavaScript methods for DOM updates.

Setting up the Development Environment

To get started with Vue.js, you need a proper development environment. Here's a step-by-step guide to setting up Vue.js:

1. **Install Node.js**: Vue.js relies on **Node.js** for its build process and package management. You can download Node.js from nodejs.org. Make sure to install the latest stable version (LTS).

2. **Install Vue CLI**: The Vue CLI (Command Line Interface) is a powerful tool for scaffolding Vue.js applications. It helps automate common development tasks, such as setting up a new project, installing dependencies, and running development servers.

To install Vue CLI, open a terminal and run the following command:

```bash
npm install -g @vue/cli
```

This command installs the Vue CLI globally on your machine.

3. **Creating a New Vue Project**: Once the Vue CLI is installed, you can create a new Vue project by running:

```bash
vue create my-vue-project
```

This will prompt you to choose a preset or manually select features like Babel, ESLint, Vuex, Vue Router, etc. For beginners, the default preset works well, and you can always customize it later.

4. **Start the Development Server**: Navigate into the project directory:

```bash
cd my-vue-project
```

Then, start the development server with:

```bash

npm run serve
```

This will launch a local server, typically running on http://localhost:8080, where you can see your Vue application in action.

5. **Install Code Editor**: A good code editor makes the development process smoother. Popular editors like **VS Code** or **Sublime Text** have plugins/extensions that enhance Vue.js development, such as syntax highlighting, autocompletion, and linting.

The Core Concepts of Vue.js

To build a strong foundation in Vue.js, it's important to understand the core concepts that form the basis of the framework. Here's an overview:

1. **The Vue Instance**: At the heart of every Vue application is the Vue instance. This is where all the data, methods, computed properties, and life-cycle hooks reside. A Vue instance can be created like this:

```javascript
```

```
const app = new Vue({
  el: '#app',
  data: {
    message: 'Hello Vue!'
  }
});
```

This binds the Vue instance to an HTML element with the id="app". The data object is reactive, meaning any changes to the data will automatically update the DOM.

2. **Directives**: Directives are special tokens in the markup that are prefixed with v-. They offer powerful functionality like conditional rendering (v-if), loops (v-for), event handling (v-on), and more.

Example:

html

```
<div v-if="isVisible">This content is visible</div>
```

3. **Components**: Components are the building blocks of a Vue application. A component is a reusable Vue instance with its own template, data, and behavior. Vue encourages a component-based architecture, where you can split your application into modular, self-contained parts.

Example:

```
javascript
```

```javascript
Vue.component('my-component', {
  template:     '<p>Hello     from     the
component!</p>'
});
```

4. **Reactivity**: Vue's reactivity system automatically updates the DOM when the data changes. You can think of it as a smart "two-way data binding" system, where the UI is always synchronized with the underlying data.

5. **Computed Properties**: Computed properties are used for reactive data transformations. Unlike methods, computed properties are cached and only recalculated when the data they depend on changes.

Example:

```
javascript
```

```javascript
computed: {
  reversedMessage() {
    return
this.message.split('').reverse().join('')
;
  }
}
```

20

6. **Vue CLI**: The Vue CLI is a command-line tool used to scaffold and manage Vue.js applications. It simplifies the development workflow, allowing you to focus more on building the application than configuring the build tools.

Summary:

In this chapter, we explored the basics of Vue.js, including what it is, why it's a great choice for front-end development, how to set up your development environment, and the core concepts that power Vue applications. With this foundation, you're ready to dive into building real-world Vue.js apps with ease. In the next chapter, we'll take a deeper look at Vue's fundamental features like templates, data binding, and directives.

CHAPTER 2

VUE.JS BASICS

Understanding the Vue Instance

The Vue instance is the core of every Vue application. It acts as the controller that connects your data (JavaScript) with your view (HTML), making the two dynamically interact. The Vue instance is essentially the entry point for all Vue.js features, and it is what enables reactivity in the application.

A Vue instance is created using the Vue constructor, like so:

```javascript
const app = new Vue({
  el: '#app',
  data: {
    message: 'Hello, Vue!'
  }
});
```

In this example:

- el specifies the HTML element that will be controlled by the Vue instance (in this case, an element with the ID app).

- `data` is an object that holds the state of your application. Any property inside the `data` object can be referenced in the template.

Vue instances are reactive, which means that when the `message` data property changes, the DOM will automatically update to reflect the new value.

The Vue instance also provides a variety of useful properties and methods, such as:

- `methods`: Defines functions that can be called in the template.
- `computed`: Defines computed properties based on the data, which are cached and recalculated only when dependent data changes.
- `watchers`: Allows you to watch for changes in a specific data property.

Template Syntax in Vue.js

Vue uses a declarative syntax, allowing you to easily bind the DOM to the underlying data. The Vue template syntax is similar to HTML but has special features that make it more interactive.

1. **Mustache Syntax**: The most common syntax is the **mustache syntax**, denoted by `{{ }}`, which is used for

23

interpolation. It allows you to bind data to the DOM easily.

Example:

```
html
```

```
<div id="app">
  <p>{{ message }}</p>
</div>
```

Here, `{{ message }}` will display the value of the `message` property from the Vue instance.

2. **Attributes Binding**: You can dynamically bind HTML attributes like `href`, `src`, `class`, etc., using the `v-bind` directive (which we'll explore in the next section).

Example:

```
html
```

```
<img v-bind:src="imageSrc" alt="Vue Logo">
```

In this case, the `src` attribute will be dynamically set to the value of `imageSrc`.

3. **Event Handling**: Vue also provides event handling capabilities via the v-on directive, allowing you to listen for events like clicks, key presses, and more.

Example:

```html
html
```

```html
<button v-on:click="changeMessage">Change Message</button>
```

In this case, the changeMessage method would be executed when the button is clicked.

4. **Shorthand Syntax**: Vue provides shorthand syntax to make templates even cleaner. For example, you can use @ as a shorthand for v-on and : for v-bind.

Example:

```html
html
```

```html
<button @click="changeMessage">Change Message</button>
<img :src="imageSrc" alt="Vue Logo">
```

Data Binding and Dynamic Rendering

One of Vue.js's most powerful features is its **reactive data binding**. When the data in a Vue instance changes, Vue

25

automatically updates the DOM to reflect those changes, ensuring that the user interface stays in sync with the application state.

1. **One-Way Data Binding**: Vue uses one-way data binding by default. This means that data flows from the Vue instance to the DOM, and changes in the Vue instance will automatically update the DOM.

    Example:

    html

    ```html
    <div id="app">
      <p>{{ message }}</p>
    </div>
    ```

    If the `message` in the Vue instance changes, the DOM will update to reflect the new value.

2. **Two-Way Data Binding with v-model**: Vue also supports **two-way data binding** with the `v-model` directive. This allows you to bind input elements (like text fields, checkboxes, etc.) to Vue data properties. Any changes made to the input will automatically update the Vue data, and vice versa.

    Example:

    html

```
<input v-model="message" placeholder="Type
a message">
<p>You typed: {{ message }}</p>
```

In this example, when the user types something in the input field, the `message` property is automatically updated in the Vue instance, and the change is reflected in the paragraph tag.

3. **Dynamic Rendering with `v-if` and `v-for`**: Vue provides directives that allow for dynamic rendering of content in the template.

   o **`v-if`**: This directive is used to conditionally render an element based on the truthiness of an expression.

   Example:

   ```
   html
   ```

   ```
   <div v-if="isVisible">This content
   is visible!</div>
   ```

   In this case, the content is displayed only if `isVisible` is `true`. If `isVisible` is `false`, the content will be removed from the DOM.

o **v-for**: This directive is used to render a list of elements based on an array or object.

Example:

html

```
<ul>
  <li     v-for="item     in     items"
:key="item.id">{{ item.name }}</li>
</ul>
```

In this example, Vue will render a list item for each item in the items array. The :key attribute is used for efficient DOM updates by uniquely identifying each list item.

Directives: v-bind, v-model, v-for, and v-if

Vue.js provides several built-in directives that you can use to manipulate DOM elements and bind them to data.

1. **v-bind**: The v-bind directive dynamically binds one or more attributes to an expression. It's commonly used for binding attributes like href, src, class, etc.

Example:

html

```
<a v-bind:href="url">Click here</a>
```

In this case, the href attribute will be dynamically set to the value of url.

2. **v-model**: The v-model directive creates two-way data bindings for form elements, allowing you to synchronize input data with the Vue instance's data properties.

Example:

html

```
<input v-model="username">
```

This binds the input field's value to the username property. If the input field is changed, the username property will be updated automatically.

3. **v-for**: The v-for directive is used to render lists by iterating over an array or object. It's similar to JavaScript's for loop but is simplified in Vue.

Example:

html

```
<ul>
```

29

```
<li       v-for="task      in      tasks"
:key="task.id">{{ task.name }}</li>
</ul>
```

This loops over the `tasks` array and displays each `task.name` in a list item.

4. **v-if**: The `v-if` directive conditionally renders elements. The element will only be inserted into the DOM if the associated expression evaluates to `true`.

   Example:

   ```
   html
   ```

   ```
   <div  v-if="showContent">This    is    some
   dynamic content</div>
   ```

   If `showContent` is `true`, the `div` will be rendered; otherwise, it will be removed from the DOM.

Summary:

In this chapter, we covered the foundational concepts of Vue.js, including the Vue instance, template syntax, and data binding. Understanding these core features will allow you to build dynamic, interactive web applications. We also explored key directives like `v-bind`, `v-model`, `v-for`, and `v-if`, which give you powerful tools for binding data and controlling the DOM in Vue.js.

In the next chapter, we will dive deeper into the Vue lifecycle and how it impacts the behavior of your applications.

CHAPTER 3

THE VUE LIFECYCLE

What is the Vue Lifecycle?

The **Vue lifecycle** refers to the series of stages or phases that a Vue instance goes through from its creation to its destruction. These stages allow developers to hook into certain points during the instance's lifecycle to execute code at specific moments. Understanding the lifecycle is crucial for managing state, side effects, and optimizing performance in Vue applications.

The Vue lifecycle consists of **creation**, **mounting**, **updating**, and **destruction**. Each stage provides hooks where developers can execute custom logic to respond to changes in the application or perform specific actions (like fetching data or cleaning up resources).

In simple terms, the Vue lifecycle defines how a Vue instance is created, updated, and destroyed. By tapping into the lifecycle hooks, developers can control what happens at different stages of the Vue instance's life.

The Different Lifecycle Hooks

Vue provides several **lifecycle hooks**, each corresponding to a specific phase of the lifecycle. These hooks allow you to run code at precise moments. They are categorized into **creation**, **mounting**, **updating**, and **destruction** phases. Let's break these down:

1. **Creation Hooks** These hooks are triggered when the Vue instance is being created.

   o **beforeCreate**: This is the first hook in the lifecycle, called before the Vue instance is created and the data is set up. It's useful for initializing non-reactive properties but is rarely used in practice.

   javascript

   ```javascript
   beforeCreate() {
     console.log('Before        create:
   instance is being created');
   }
   ```

   o **created**: This hook is called right after the Vue instance has been created and the data has been initialized. At this point, you can access the data, computed properties, and methods, but the DOM has not yet been mounted.

   javascript

   ```javascript
   created() {
   ```

33

```
console.log('Created:    Data    is
available, but DOM is not mounted');
}
```

2. **Mounting Hooks** These hooks are triggered when the Vue instance is mounted to the DOM.

    o   **beforeMount**: This hook is called right before the Vue instance is mounted to the DOM. It's used to perform any last-minute preparations before the DOM is rendered.

    ```
    javascript
    ```

    ```
    beforeMount() {
      console.log('Before          mount:
    instance is about to be mounted');
    }
    ```

    o   **mounted**: This is called after the instance has been mounted to the DOM. This is the point where you can safely interact with the DOM or fetch data from an external source. It's often used for fetching data asynchronously.

    ```
    javascript
    ```

    ```
    mounted() {
      console.log('Mounted: instance has
    been mounted to the DOM');
    ```

34

}

3. **Updating Hooks** These hooks are triggered whenever the data changes, causing the view to be re-rendered.

   o **beforeUpdate**: This hook is called when reactive data changes, but before the DOM is updated. It gives you a chance to react to data changes before they are reflected in the UI.

   ```javascript
   beforeUpdate() {
     console.log('Before update: data is changing');
   }
   ```

   o **updated**: This hook is called after the DOM has been updated. It allows you to access the DOM after Vue has re-rendered the view.

   ```javascript
   updated() {
     console.log('Updated: the DOM has been updated');
   }
   ```

4. **Destruction Hooks** These hooks are triggered when the Vue instance is being destroyed, typically when navigating away from a component or page.

   o **beforeDestroy**: This hook is called right before a Vue instance is destroyed. It's useful for cleaning up resources, such as canceling network requests, clearing timers, or removing event listeners.

   javascript

   ```javascript
   beforeDestroy() {
     console.log('Before        destroy:
   instance is about to be destroyed');
   }
   ```

   o **destroyed**: This hook is called after the instance has been destroyed. This is the last moment you can perform cleanup tasks like releasing resources.

   javascript

   ```javascript
   destroyed() {
     console.log('Destroyed:     instance
   has been destroyed');
   }
   ```

36

Practical Use Cases for Lifecycle Hooks

Now that we have a good understanding of the lifecycle hooks, let's look at some practical use cases where these hooks can be effectively used in Vue.js applications.

1. **Fetching Data from an API (Mounted Hook)** One of the most common use cases for the `mounted` hook is fetching data from an external API. When a component is mounted, we can use this hook to trigger an API request and update the component's state.

    ```javascript
    mounted() {
      // Fetching data when the component is mounted
      fetch('https://api.example.com/data')
        .then(response => response.json())
        .then(data => {
          this.items = data;
        })
        .catch(error => {
          console.error('Error        fetching
    data:', error);
        });
    }
    ```

In this example, the component fetches data from an API when it's mounted and stores the data in the `items` array. The UI will automatically update once the data is fetched.

2. **Setting Up Event Listeners (Created/Destroyed Hooks)** Sometimes, you need to add custom event listeners to the window or document. The `created` hook is a great place to set this up, and the `destroyed` hook is used to clean up after the component is destroyed.

```javascript
created() {
  // Adding a global event listener
  window.addEventListener('resize',
this.handleResize);
},
destroyed() {
  // Removing the event listener when the
component is destroyed
  window.removeEventListener('resize',
this.handleResize);
},
methods: {
  handleResize() {
    console.log('Window resized');
  }
}
```

This ensures that the event listener is added when the component is created and removed when the component is destroyed, preventing memory leaks.

3. **Tracking Changes in Data (BeforeUpdate/Updated Hooks)** If you need to perform actions based on changes in data, the `beforeUpdate` and `updated` hooks are ideal. For example, you might want to track how many times a user clicks a button and show a message after a certain number of clicks.

```javascript

data() {
  return {
    clickCount: 0
  };
},
beforeUpdate() {
  // Can be used to track data changes
before the UI updates
  console.log('Before    update:    current
click count', this.clickCount);
},
updated() {
  // You can perform actions after the DOM
updates
  if (this.clickCount >= 5) {
    alert('You clicked 5 times!');
```

```
    }
  },
  methods: {
    incrementClickCount() {
      this.clickCount++;
    }
  }
```

In this case, every time the button is clicked, the `clickCount` will be updated. If the count reaches 5, an alert is shown.

4. **Cleanup (BeforeDestroy Hook)** When components are removed from the DOM, it's essential to clean up resources like network requests, intervals, or timeouts to avoid memory leaks. The `beforeDestroy` hook is perfect for this task.

javascript

```
beforeDestroy() {
  clearInterval(this.timer);
},
created() {
  // Set an interval when the component is
created
  this.timer = setInterval(() => {
    console.log('Timer running...');
  }, 1000);
```

```
}
```

In this example, a timer is set up when the component is created and cleared when the component is about to be destroyed, ensuring that the timer doesn't continue running after the component is removed.

5. **Handling User Authentication (Mounted Hook)** For apps that involve user authentication, you may want to check whether the user is logged in when a page is loaded. The mounted hook can be used for this task.

javascript

```
mounted() {
  // Check if the user is authenticated
  if (!this.isAuthenticated()) {
    this.$router.push('/login');
  }
},
methods: {
  isAuthenticated() {
    return
localStorage.getItem('auth_token')     !==
null;
  }
}
```

Here, the app checks if a user is authenticated when the component is mounted. If not, it redirects the user to the login page.

Summary:

In this chapter, we explored the Vue.js lifecycle and the various lifecycle hooks that allow you to control your Vue instance at different stages. From creation and mounting to updates and destruction, these hooks give you fine-grained control over your components and provide opportunities to handle tasks such as data fetching, event handling, and resource cleanup.

By mastering the Vue lifecycle and understanding when to use these hooks, you can build more efficient, maintainable, and optimized Vue applications. In the next chapter, we will dive deeper into Vue components, which are the core building blocks of any Vue.js application.

CHAPTER 4

VUE COMPONENTS: THE BUILDING BLOCKS

What are Vue Components?

In Vue.js, **components** are the fundamental building blocks of your application. They are reusable, self-contained units that allow you to split the user interface (UI) into smaller, manageable pieces. A component can be as simple as a button or as complex as an entire page of your app. Each component has its own template, logic, and style, which makes the code more modular and easier to maintain.

Vue components make it easier to structure large applications because you can break down complex UIs into smaller, reusable pieces. Components can be nested within one another, which provides a powerful and flexible way to build dynamic applications.

A basic component consists of:

- **Template**: The HTML structure of the component.
- **Script**: The logic, including data, methods, computed properties, and lifecycle hooks.
- **Style**: The scoped CSS specific to that component.

43

Vue components can be created either **locally** or **globally**.

Creating and Registering Components

Local Components:

Local components are defined and used within a specific parent component. They are registered inside the parent component's components option.

Example of creating and registering a local component:

```javascript
// Parent component (App.vue)
<template>
  <div>
    <h1>Welcome to Vue.js</h1>
    <custom-button></custom-button>   <!-- Using
the local component -->
  </div>
</template>

<script>
// Import the child component
import CustomButton from './CustomButton.vue';

export default {
  components: {
```

```
    CustomButton // Registering the component
locally
  }
}
</script>
javascript
```

```
// Child component (CustomButton.vue)
<template>
  <button>Click Me</button>
</template>

<script>
export default {
  name: 'CustomButton' // Optional, but good
practice to name the component
}
</script>

<style scoped>
button {
  background-color: blue;
  color: white;
  padding: 10px;
}
</style>
```

In this example, the `CustomButton` component is registered inside the parent component's `components` object and then used in the template. This is a local registration method.

Global Components:

Global components are registered once, typically in the main entry file, and can be used anywhere within the Vue application.

Example of registering a global component:

javascript

```
// main.js (Entry file)
import Vue from 'vue';
import App from './App.vue';
import                CustomButton                from
'./components/CustomButton.vue';

// Registering the component globally
Vue.component('custom-button', CustomButton);

new Vue({
  render: h => h(App),
}).$mount('#app');
```

With global registration, the `CustomButton` component is available throughout the entire application without needing to import it into each parent component.

Prop Passing and Event Emitting

One of the key features of Vue components is the ability to **pass data** between them. This is done using **props** and **events**.

Passing Data with Props:

Props allow parent components to pass data to child components. This is how data is communicated from the parent to the child. A prop is a custom attribute that you define in the child component, and it can accept any type of data, such as strings, numbers, arrays, objects, or even functions.

Example of passing a prop:

```javascript
// Parent component (App.vue)
<template>
  <div>
    <custom-button :label="buttonText"></custom-button> <!-- Passing data to child -->
  </div>
</template>

<script>
import CustomButton from './CustomButton.vue';

export default {
```

```
    components: {
      CustomButton
    },
    data() {
      return {
        buttonText: 'Click Me'
      };
    }
  }
</script>
javascript

// Child component (CustomButton.vue)
<template>
  <button>{{ label }}</button> <!-- Using the
passed prop -->
</template>

<script>
export default {
  props: ['label'] // Declare the prop
}
</script>
```

In this example, the buttonText data from the parent is passed to the child CustomButton component via the label prop. The child component then renders the label inside a <button>.

Event Emitting (Communication from Child to Parent):

In Vue, child components can send data back to their parent components by emitting custom events. To do this, you use the `this.$emit` method, which allows the child to trigger an event on the parent.

Example of emitting an event:

javascript

```
// Parent component (App.vue)
<template>
  <div>
    <custom-button
@clicked="handleClick"></custom-button>     <!--
Listening for event -->
  </div>
</template>

<script>
import CustomButton from './CustomButton.vue';

export default {
  components: {
    CustomButton
  },
  methods: {
    handleClick(message) {
```

```
      console.log('Button clicked:', message);
   }
  }
}
</script>
javascript
```

```
// Child component (CustomButton.vue)
<template>
  <button          @click="clickHandler">Click
Me</button> <!-- Emitting the event on click -->
</template>
```

```
<script>
export default {
  methods: {
    clickHandler() {
      // Emitting the custom event to the parent
with data
      this.$emit('clicked',      'Hello      from
child!');
    }
  }
}
</script>
```

In this case, when the button in the CustomButton component is clicked, the child emits a clicked event, passing the string 'Hello from child!' as data to the parent. The parent listens for this event using `@clicked="handleClick"`, and the `handleClick` method logs the message.

Scoped Slots and Dynamic Components

Scoped Slots:

Scoped slots are a powerful feature in Vue that allows the child component to expose part of its internal data to the parent component, making the parent able to customize the child component's content. Scoped slots are particularly useful when you want to create highly reusable components that offer customization options for their content.

Example of using a scoped slot:

javascript

```
// Parent component (App.vue)
<template>
  <div>
    <custom-card>
      <template v-slot:header>
        <h1>Custom Header</h1>
      </template>
      <template v-slot:default>
        <p>This is some custom content in the
card.</p>
      </template>
    </custom-card>
```

```
    </div>
</template>

<script>
import CustomCard from './CustomCard.vue';

export default {
  components: {
    CustomCard
  }
}
</script>
javascript

// Child component (CustomCard.vue)
<template>
  <div class="card">
    <div class="card-header">
      <slot name="header">Default Header</slot>
<!-- Scoped slot -->
    </div>
    <div class="card-body">
      <slot>Default Content</slot> <!-- Default
slot -->
    </div>
  </div>
</template>

<script>
```

```
export default {
  name: 'CustomCard'
}
</script>
```

In this example, the parent component provides custom content to the `header` and `default` slots of the `CustomCard` component. The child component can then render the content provided by the parent. If the parent doesn't provide any content, the child uses the default content (`Default Header` and `Default Content`).

Dynamic Components:

Dynamic components allow you to render different components conditionally within a single parent component. Vue provides the `<component>` tag, which can be used to dynamically switch between components based on some data or condition.

Example of using dynamic components:

javascript

```
<template>
  <div>
    <button     @click="currentComponent    =
'componentA'">Load Component A</button>
    <button     @click="currentComponent    =
'componentB'">Load Component B</button>
```

53

```
    <component
:is="currentComponent"></component>          <!--
Dynamically render components -->
  </div>
</template>

<script>
import ComponentA from './ComponentA.vue';
import ComponentB from './ComponentB.vue';

export default {
  data() {
    return {
      currentComponent: 'componentA'
    };
  },
  components: {
    componentA: ComponentA,
    componentB: ComponentB
  }
}
</script>
```

In this case, clicking on a button dynamically changes the currentComponent data, which updates the rendered component. The <component :is="currentComponent"> tag uses the currentComponent value to determine which component to render.

Summary:

In this chapter, we explored the concept of **Vue components**, which are the building blocks of any Vue application. We learned how to create and register components locally and globally, pass data between components using props, and communicate between components using custom events. Additionally, we covered advanced features like **scoped slots**, which allow for dynamic content in child components, and **dynamic components**, which let you conditionally render components based on application data.

In the next chapter, we'll dive deeper into **Vue.js Directives** and learn how to use them to enhance our templates with dynamic behavior.

CHAPTER 5

WORKING WITH VUE DIRECTIVES

Overview of Directives in Vue

In Vue.js, **directives** are special tokens in the markup that bind behavior to DOM elements. They are prefixed with v- to distinguish them from regular HTML attributes. Directives offer Vue.js its reactive and declarative nature, enabling dynamic behavior in the DOM.

Directives in Vue work by modifying the DOM when the data changes. They are a powerful tool for managing DOM rendering and behavior, making your Vue components more flexible and dynamic.

Vue has several built-in directives, such as v-if, v-for, v-bind, v-model, and others, that provide common functionalities. However, Vue also allows you to create your own custom directives to handle specific needs or behaviors within your application.

Custom Directives: Creating and Using Them

Vue allows developers to create **custom directives** for specific use cases. Custom directives give you the ability to define reusable functionality that can be applied to DOM elements.

Creating a Custom Directive

To create a custom directive, you use the `Vue.directive()` method. The basic syntax is:

javascript

```javascript
Vue.directive('my-directive', {
  // Hook functions: bind, inserted, update, unbind
  bind(el, binding) {
    // Directly modify the DOM element
    el.style.color = binding.value;
  }
});
```

In this example, we're creating a custom directive `v-my-directive` that changes the text color of the element it is applied to. The directive accepts a value (`binding.value`), which represents the color to apply.

Using the Custom Directive

Once the custom directive is defined, you can apply it in your component template using `v-<directive-name>`.

Example of using the custom directive:

html

```
<template>
  <div v-my-directive="'blue'">
    This text will be blue.
  </div>
</template>
```

In this example, the text inside the `<div>` will be rendered in blue because we applied the custom `v-my-directive` directive, passing `'blue'` as the value.

Common Lifecycle Hooks for Custom Directives

Custom directives in Vue support various lifecycle hooks that allow you to interact with the DOM at different stages of the element's lifecycle. These hooks are:

1. **`bind(el, binding)`**: Called when the directive is first bound to the element. This is where you can initialize things.

2. **inserted(el)**: Called when the element is inserted into the DOM. Useful for post-processing the DOM element.

3. **update(el, binding)**: Called when the bound element's value changes. It's ideal for reacting to changes in the directive.

4. **componentUpdated(el, binding)**: Similar to update, but called after the component's DOM has been re-rendered.

5. **unbind(el)**: Called when the directive is unbound from the element. It's useful for cleanup.

Example using multiple hooks in a custom directive:

javascript

```javascript
Vue.directive('highlight', {
  bind(el) {
    el.style.backgroundColor = 'yellow';
  },
  unbind(el) {
    el.style.backgroundColor = '';
  }
});
```

In this example, the custom directive v-highlight will apply a yellow background color to the element when it's bound, and remove it when the directive is unbound.

Common Built-In Directives

Vue.js comes with several powerful built-in directives that you'll use frequently when building applications. Here's a look at some of the most commonly used ones:

1. **v-if**: The v-if directive conditionally renders elements. The element will only be added to the DOM if the expression evaluates to true. If the expression is false, the element is removed.

   Example:

   html

   ```
   <div v-if="isVisible">This content is visible</div>
   ```

   In this case, the div will only appear if the isVisible property is true. If it's false, the element is removed from the DOM.

2. **v-for**: The v-for directive is used to loop through arrays or objects and render a list of elements. It's similar to a for loop in JavaScript.

   Example:

   html

```
<ul>
  <li     v-for="item     in     items"
:key="item.id">{{ item.name }}</li>
</ul>
```

Here, the `v-for` directive iterates through the `items` array and renders an `li` element for each item.

3. **v-bind**: The `v-bind` directive binds an attribute to an expression. It is often used to dynamically bind HTML attributes like `href`, `src`, `class`, and more.

Example:

```
html
```

```
<img   v-bind:src="imageUrl"   alt="Vue.js
Logo">
```

This binds the `src` attribute of the `<img>` tag to the `imageUrl` property in the Vue instance, dynamically updating the image source.

4. **v-model**: The `v-model` directive creates a two-way data binding between an input element and the Vue instance's data. It's commonly used with form elements like `input`, `textarea`, and `select`.

61

Example:

```
html
```

```
<input v-model="message" placeholder="Type something">
```

This binds the input field's value to the `message` data property. Any changes in the input will update the `message` value, and vice versa.

5. **v-show**: The `v-show` directive is similar to `v-if`, but instead of removing the element from the DOM, it only toggles the element's visibility using CSS (`display: none`).

Example:

```
html
```

```
<div v-show="isVisible">This content is visible</div>
```

In this case, the `div` will be hidden or shown based on the `isVisible` property, but the element will remain in the DOM.

6. **v-on**: The `v-on` directive is used to listen to DOM events and execute methods when those events are triggered.

Example:

html

```
<button    v-on:click="handleClick">Click
Me</button>
```

This listens for a click event on the button and executes the `handleClick` method when clicked. You can also use shorthand for `v-on`, like `@click`.

Practical Example: Building a Dynamic List with Directives

Let's use the power of Vue directives to build a simple dynamic list that allows the user to add and remove items. This will demonstrate the use of `v-if`, `v-for`, `v-bind`, and `v-model`.

Step-by-Step Example

1. **Template**: Create a list that displays items from an array, allows adding new items, and removes items with a button click.

html

```
<template>
  <div>
    <input v-model="newItem" placeholder="Add a
new item">
```

```
<button @click="addItem">Add Item</button>

<ul>
  <li  v-for="(item,  index)  in  items"
:key="index">
    {{ item }}
    <button
@click="removeItem(index)">Remove</button>
  </li>
  </ul>
  </div>
</template>
```

2. **Script**: Define the data and methods that manage the list and handle user input.

javascript

```
<script>
export default {
  data() {
    return {
      newItem: '',
      items: []
    };
  },
  methods: {
    addItem() {
      if (this.newItem.trim()) {
        this.items.push(this.newItem);
```

```
        this.newItem = ''; // Clear the input
field
    }
  },
  removeItem(index) {
    this.items.splice(index, 1); // Remove the
item at the given index
    }
  }
};
</script>
```

3. **Explanation**:

   o **v-for**: Loops through the items array and renders a list item (`<li>`) for each element. The :key attribute is used to uniquely identify each item, which improves performance when Vue updates the DOM.

   o **v-model**: Binds the input field to the newItem property, allowing two-way data binding.

   o **@click**: Listens for click events on the buttons and triggers the corresponding methods (addItem and removeItem).

   o **v-bind**: Can be used if you need to bind dynamic attributes like class, style, etc. In this example, it's not explicitly required, but it can be added if needed.

Summary:

In this chapter, we explored how **Vue directives** provide a powerful way to bind dynamic behavior to DOM elements. We covered common built-in directives such as `v-if`, `v-for`, `v-bind`, `v-model`, and `v-on`, as well as how to create and use **custom directives** to address unique application needs.

We also built a practical example of a dynamic list, demonstrating how Vue's directives can be used together to create interactive, data-driven applications. In the next chapter, we will dive deeper into **computed properties** and **watchers**, which offer additional ways to handle dynamic data in Vue.js.

CHAPTER 6

DATA BINDING IN VUE

What is Data Binding?

Data binding is a mechanism that allows you to bind the values of the application's data (the JavaScript state) to the elements of the user interface (HTML). With Vue.js, data binding provides a way to keep your DOM and data in sync automatically. This makes the application more interactive and responsive because the user interface updates whenever the data changes.

Vue offers two primary types of data binding: **one-way** and **two-way**.

- **One-way binding** allows data to flow in one direction, from the Vue instance's data to the view (the DOM).
- **Two-way binding** allows data to flow both ways: changes in the DOM (such as user input) automatically update the Vue data, and changes in the Vue data automatically update the DOM.

Vue makes data binding intuitive and simple, and you can apply it to HTML attributes, text, form inputs, and more.

One-Way and Two-Way Data Binding

One-Way Data Binding

One-way data binding refers to the flow of data from the Vue instance (data object) to the DOM. This means that any change in the data will automatically update the view, but changes in the view (UI) do not affect the underlying data unless explicitly done through an event handler.

The most common form of one-way binding in Vue is using the **mustache syntax** {{ }} for rendering data in the template.

Example of one-way data binding with mustache syntax:

html

```
<template>
  <div>
    <p>{{ message }}</p>    <!-- The message
property is displayed -->
  </div>
</template>

<script>
export default {
  data() {
    return {
      message: 'Hello, Vue!'
    };
```

```
    }
}
</script>
```

Here, the value of `message` is bound to the DOM, so whenever `message` changes in the Vue instance, the displayed content will automatically update.

Two-Way Data Binding

Two-way data binding allows data to be bound in both directions: if the data in the Vue instance changes, the view updates; and if the user changes the input, the Vue data is updated as well. This is particularly useful for form elements like text inputs, checkboxes, and select dropdowns.

Vue uses the **v-model directive** to create two-way data binding. This allows you to bind input elements to Vue data properties, automatically keeping them in sync.

Example of two-way data binding with `v-model`:

html

```
<template>
  <div>
    <input  v-model="message"  placeholder="Type
something"> <!-- Two-way binding -->
```

```
  <p>You    typed:    {{   message   }}</p>   <!--
Displaying the value of message -->
  </div>
</template>

<script>
export default {
  data() {
    return {
      message: ''  // This  will  automatically
update when the user types
    };
  }
}
</script>
```

In this example, the input field is bound to the `message` data property. Any changes made by the user will instantly update the `message` property, and the displayed paragraph (`<p>`) will reflect those changes in real time.

Using v-model for Forms and Input Elements

Vue's `v-model` directive simplifies handling form inputs, enabling seamless two-way data binding between the form element and the Vue instance's data. It can be used with various form elements, including text inputs, checkboxes, radio buttons, and select dropdowns.

Using v-model with Text Inputs

The `v-model` directive can be used to bind a text input to a data property. Any user input will automatically update the bound property.

Example with a text input:

html

```
<template>
  <div>
    <input v-model="username" placeholder="Enter your username">
    <p>Your username is: {{ username }}</p>
  </div>
</template>

<script>
export default {
  data() {
    return {
      username: ''
    };
  }
}
</script>
```

Here, the username data property is bound to the input field, and any text entered by the user will be reflected in the data property and the paragraph tag.

Using v-model with Checkboxes

With checkboxes, v-model binds the checkbox's checked state to a data property. If the checkbox is checked, the value will be updated; if unchecked, the value will revert.

Example with a checkbox:

html

```html
<template>
  <div>
    <input type="checkbox" v-model="isChecked">
I agree to the terms and conditions
    <p>Agreement status: {{ isChecked }}</p>
  </div>
</template>

<script>
export default {
  data() {
    return {
      isChecked: false
    };
  }
```

```
}
</script>
```

In this case, `isChecked` is a Boolean value that is bound to the checkbox. If the checkbox is checked, the `isChecked` property will be `true`, and if it is unchecked, it will be `false`.

Using v-model with Radio Buttons

For radio buttons, `v-model` binds a group of radio buttons to a single data property. The selected radio button's value will update the bound property.

Example with radio buttons:

html

```
<template>
  <div>
    <label>
      <input    type="radio"    v-model="picked"
value="Option A"> Option A
    </label>
    <label>
      <input    type="radio"    v-model="picked"
value="Option B"> Option B
    </label>
    <p>You picked: {{ picked }}</p>
  </div>
```

```
</template>

<script>
export default {
  data() {
    return {
      picked: 'Option A'  // Default value
    };
  }
}
</script>
```

Here, the `picked` property is bound to the selected radio button. If the user selects "Option B", the `picked` value will update to reflect the selection.

Using v-model with Select Dropdowns

You can use `v-model` with `<select>` elements to create dynamic drop-down menus. The selected value is automatically bound to the specified data property.

Example with a dropdown:

html

```
<template>
  <div>
    <select v-model="selectedOption">
```

```
      <option  disabled  value="">Please  select
one</option>
      <option>Option 1</option>
      <option>Option 2</option>
      <option>Option 3</option>
    </select>
    <p>You selected: {{ selectedOption }}</p>
  </div>
</template>

<script>
export default {
  data() {
    return {
      selectedOption: ''
    };
  }
}
</script>
```

In this example, selectedOption is bound to the dropdown. The value of selectedOption will update whenever the user selects a different option from the dropdown.

Real-World Example: Creating a Simple Form

Let's build a simple form that captures user input and displays it dynamically as the user fills it out. The form will include text

75

inputs, a checkbox, radio buttons, and a select dropdown, all of which will use `v-model` for two-way data binding.

html

```
<template>
  <div>
    <h1>User Registration Form</h1>

    <form @submit.prevent="submitForm">
      <div>
        <label for="username">Username:</label>
        <input        v-model="formData.username"
id="username"  type="text"   placeholder="Enter
username" required>
      </div>

      <div>
        <label for="email">Email:</label>
        <input         v-model="formData.email"
id="email"     type="email"   placeholder="Enter
email" required>
      </div>

      <div>
        <label>
          <input        type="checkbox"        v-
model="formData.agreeToTerms"> I  agree  to  the
terms and conditions
```

```
        </label>
      </div>


      <div>
        <label>Gender:</label>
        <label>
          <input          type="radio"        v-
model="formData.gender" value="Male"> Male
        </label>
        <label>
          <input          type="radio"        v-
model="formData.gender" value="Female"> Female
        </label>
      </div>


      <div>
        <label for="country">Country:</label>
        <select        v-model="formData.country"
id="country" required>
          <option    value="">Please    select    a
country</option>
          <option>USA</option>
          <option>Canada</option>
          <option>UK</option>
        </select>
      </div>


      <button type="submit">Submit</button>
    </form>
```

```
    <h2>Form Data</h2>
    <p>Username: {{ formData.username }}</p>
    <p>Email: {{ formData.email }}</p>
    <p>Terms Accepted: {{ formData.agreeToTerms
? 'Yes' : 'No' }}</p>
    <p>Gender: {{ formData.gender }}</p>
    <p>Country: {{ formData.country }}</p>
  </div>
</template>

<script>
export default {
  data() {
    return {
      formData: {
        username: '',
        email: '',
        agreeToTerms: false,
        gender: '',
        country: ''
      }
    };
  },
  methods: {
    submitForm() {
      console.log('Form                submitted:',
this.formData);
    }
```

```
    }
}
</script>
```

In this form:

- The `v-model` directive binds the form elements to the `formData` object.
- As the user fills in the form, the `formData` object updates in real-time.
- When the form is submitted, the data is logged to the console.

Summary:

In this chapter, we explored **data binding** in Vue.js and discussed the two primary types: **one-way** and **two-way** data binding. We examined how to use the `v-model` directive for forms and input elements, allowing us to easily synchronize the DOM with Vue's data. Finally, we built a simple form to demonstrate real-world use cases for Vue's data binding features.

In the next chapter, we will explore **computed properties** and **watchers**, which provide powerful tools for reacting to data changes and optimizing performance.

CHAPTER 7

EVENT HANDLING IN VUE.JS

Handling Events in Vue

Event handling is an essential feature in any web application, and Vue.js makes it straightforward to attach event listeners to DOM elements. In Vue, events are handled using the **v-on** directive, which is used to listen to DOM events like clicks, mouse movements, keyboard actions, and more.

Vue's event system is flexible, providing several ways to manage event listeners. By binding event listeners to the DOM elements, you can trigger methods, update state, and respond to user actions in an efficient way.

Vue also offers modifiers and custom event handling, making it easier to manage events and tailor their behavior to the specific needs of your application.

Using v-on for Event Listeners

The **v-on** directive is used to listen for events and execute methods when those events are triggered. It's shorthand for adding event listeners in Vue, enabling you to easily handle DOM events such as clicks, key presses, form submissions, etc.

The basic syntax for using `v-on`:

html

```
<button          v-on:click="handleClick">Click
Me</button>
```

In this example, when the button is clicked, the `handleClick` method will be executed.

Shorthand Syntax for v-on

Vue also provides a shorthand for the `v-on` directive. Instead of writing `v-on:event`, you can use the @ symbol.

For example:

html

```
<button @click="handleClick">Click Me</button>
```

This shorthand syntax is more concise and is commonly used in Vue applications.

Binding Event Handlers to Methods

You can bind event listeners to Vue methods. These methods can be defined inside the `methods` object of the Vue instance. When the event is triggered, Vue will call the corresponding method.

Example:

html

```
<template>
  <div>
    <button          @click="changeMessage">Click
Me</button>
    <p>{{ message }}</p>
  </div>
</template>

<script>
export default {
  data() {
    return {
      message: 'Hello, Vue!'
    };
  },
  methods: {
    changeMessage() {
      this.message = 'You clicked the button!';
    }
  }
};
</script>
```

In this example, when the button is clicked, the `changeMessage` method is called, which updates the `message` data property. The paragraph tag (`<p>`) then reflects the updated message.

Modifiers for Events

Vue provides **event modifiers** that allow you to manage events more efficiently. Modifiers are special symbols that can be added to the event listener to modify its behavior. These modifiers provide an easy way to handle common scenarios, such as preventing the default behavior, stopping the event propagation, and capturing events.

Here are some of the most commonly used event modifiers:

1. **.prevent**: Prevents the default behavior of the event.

   Example:

   html

   ```
   <form
   @submit.prevent="handleSubmit">Submit</fo
   rm>
   ```

   The `.prevent` modifier prevents the form from being submitted to the server and triggers the `handleSubmit` method instead.

2. **.stop**: Stops the event from propagating up the DOM tree (stops event bubbling).

Example:

html

```
<button    @click.stop="handleClick">Click
Me</button>
```

In this case, .stop prevents the click event from propagating to any parent elements.

3. **.capture**: Listens for events during the capturing phase instead of the bubbling phase.

Example:

html

```
<button @click.capture="handleClick">Click
Me</button>
```

This modifier ensures that the click event is handled during the capturing phase, which is triggered before the event bubbles up the DOM.

4. **.once**: Ensures the event listener is triggered only once.

Example:

```
html
```

```
<button    @click.once="handleClick">Click
Me</button>
```

With .once, the handleClick method will only be executed once when the button is clicked. After that, the event listener is removed.

5. **.native**: When using custom components, .native can be used to listen to native DOM events, such as click or input, instead of Vue's custom events.

Example:

```
html
```

```
<custom-button
@click.native="handleClick">Click
Me</custom-button>
```

This will trigger the handleClick method when the native click event occurs on the custom-button component.

Practical Example: Creating Interactive Buttons and Forms

Let's create a small interactive form with buttons that utilize Vue.js event handling, including different event modifiers to manage user interactions.

Step-by-Step Example

We will create a simple form where users can input their name, and a button will trigger a greeting message. Additionally, we'll have a button that demonstrates how to use the `.stop` modifier to stop event propagation.

1. **Template**: Create the HTML structure with buttons and an input field.

html

```
<template>
  <div>
    <h1>Interactive Form</h1>

    <!-- Name input -->
    <input      v-model="name"      type="text"
placeholder="Enter your name">

    <!-- Button with regular event handler -->
    <button @click="greetUser">Greet Me</button>
```

```
    <!-- Button with event modifier to stop
propagation -->
    <button @click.stop="logClick">Click Me (No
Propagation)</button>


    <!-- Displaying the greeting -->
    <p>{{ greeting }}</p>
  </div>
</template>
```

2. **Script**: Define the data properties and methods for handling the events.

```javascript
<script>
export default {
  data() {
    return {
      name: '',  // User input
      greeting: ''  // Greeting message
    };
  },
  methods: {
    // Method to greet the user
    greetUser() {
      if (this.name.trim()) {
        this.greeting = `Hello, ${this.name}!`;
      } else {
```

```
        this.greeting  =  'Please  enter  your
name.';
    }
  },
  // Method for logging click event (with
propagation stopped)
    logClick() {
      console.log('Button clicked');
    }
  }
};
</script>
```

3. **Explanation**:
   - o **v-model**: Binds the name input field to the `name` data property, enabling two-way data binding.
   - o **Regular button**: When the "Greet Me" button is clicked, the `greetUser` method updates the `greeting` data property based on the input value.
   - o **Button with .stop modifier**: When the "Click Me (No Propagation)" button is clicked, the `logClick` method logs a message, and the `.stop` modifier prevents the event from propagating further up the DOM (e.g., preventing parent elements from responding to the click event).

88

- o **Greeting**: Displays a dynamic greeting message based on the user's input.

4. **Result**:
    - o When the user types their name and clicks "Greet Me", they receive a personalized greeting.
    - o Clicking "Click Me (No Propagation)" logs a message to the console but prevents any parent element from reacting to the click event.

Summary:

In this chapter, we explored **event handling** in Vue.js, focusing on how to use the `v-on` directive to listen for and respond to events. We learned about **event modifiers** like `.prevent`, `.stop`, `.once`, `.capture`, and `.native`, which allow us to control the behavior of events in Vue applications. These modifiers help manage event propagation, prevent default actions, and handle events more flexibly.

Finally, we built a simple **interactive form** with buttons, using Vue's event handling features to demonstrate how to create dynamic, responsive UIs. In the next chapter, we will dive into **computed properties** and **watchers**, which provide powerful tools for managing and responding to data changes.

CHAPTER 8

COMPUTED PROPERTIES AND WATCHERS

Understanding Computed Properties

In Vue.js, **computed properties** are functions that return a value based on the component's data. The key feature of computed properties is that they are **cached** based on their dependencies, meaning they will only recompute when the data they depend on changes.

Computed properties are especially useful when you need to perform transformations or calculations on your data and want to avoid unnecessary recalculations. Instead of recalculating a value every time the component re-renders, Vue.js will only recompute it when the relevant data changes.

Example of a Computed Property

Here's a simple example of a computed property that combines the first name and last name into a full name:

html

```
<template>
```

```
<div>
  <p>Full Name: {{ fullName }}</p>
</div>
</template>

<script>
export default {
  data() {
    return {
      firstName: 'John',
      lastName: 'Doe'
    };
  },
  computed: {
    fullName() {
      return                    `${this.firstName}
${this.lastName}`;
    }
  }
};
</script>
```

In this example, `fullName` is a computed property. Whenever `firstName` or `lastName` changes, Vue will recompute the `fullName` property. Vue ensures that this property is only recalculated when its dependencies (`firstName` and `lastName`) change, improving performance by avoiding unnecessary recalculations.

How Computed Properties Improve Performance

Computed properties offer significant performance benefits compared to using methods for data transformations or calculations. The main advantage is **caching**: computed properties are cached based on their dependencies, which means they are only recalculated when their dependencies actually change. This prevents unnecessary calculations when the data has not changed.

Why Use Computed Properties Instead of Methods?

If you use a method to perform a transformation or calculation, the method will be executed every time the component re-renders, even if the data has not changed. This can be inefficient, especially for complex or expensive operations.

Example using a method (inefficient):

html

```
<template>
  <div>
    <p>Full Name: {{ getFullName() }}</p>
  </div>
</template>

<script>
export default {
  data() {
```

```
  return {
    firstName: 'John',
    lastName: 'Doe'
  };
},
methods: {
  getFullName() {
    return                    `${this.firstName}
${this.lastName}`;
  }
}
};
</script>
```

In this case, the `getFullName()` method will be called every time the component re-renders, even if `firstName` and `lastName` haven't changed. This can be wasteful in scenarios where performance is a concern.

In contrast, using a computed property ensures that the full name is only recalculated when `firstName` or `lastName` changes.

The Role of Watchers in Vue.js

While computed properties are ideal for calculations or transformations based on reactive data, **watchers** are used to perform side effects or asynchronous tasks in response to data changes.

A **watcher** allows you to observe specific data properties and react when those properties change. Watchers are particularly useful for scenarios where you need to execute logic, such as making an API call or performing an expensive operation, in response to a change in data.

When to Use Watchers

- When you need to perform an action in response to data changes (e.g., API calls, validation, side effects).
- When you need to watch for deep changes in an object or array.
- When you want to track multiple data properties and perform a custom action when any of them changes.

Basic Example of a Watcher

Here's an example of a watcher that reacts when the `message` data property changes:

html

```html
<template>
  <div>
    <input  v-model="message"  placeholder="Type something">
    <p>Message: {{ message }}</p>
  </div>
```

```
</template>

<script>
export default {
  data() {
    return {
      message: ''
    };
  },
  watch: {
    message(newValue) {
      console.log('Message      changed      to:',
newValue);
    }
  }
};
</script>
```

In this example:

- A watcher is set up on the `message` property.
- Every time `message` changes, the watcher logs the new value to the console.

Watching Deep Changes

For complex objects or arrays, you can use the `deep` option to watch for nested changes.

Example:

```javascript
watch: {
  'user.address.city': {
    handler(newValue) {
      console.log('City changed to:', newValue);
    },
    deep: true
  }
}
```

This will watch for any change in the `user.address.city` property, even if the change occurs deep within an object.

Real-World Example: Building a Calculator App

Let's build a simple calculator app that demonstrates both **computed properties** and **watchers**. The app will allow the user to input numbers and perform basic arithmetic operations.

1. **Template**: Create input fields and buttons for the calculator.

```html
<template>
  <div>
```

```
<h1>Simple Calculator</h1>
<input    v-model="number1"    type="number"
placeholder="Enter first number">
<input    v-model="number2"    type="number"
placeholder="Enter second number">

<div>
   <button          @click="operation      =
'add'">Add</button>
   <button          @click="operation      =
'subtract'">Subtract</button>
   <button          @click="operation      =
'multiply'">Multiply</button>
   <button          @click="operation      =
'divide'">Divide</button>
  </div>

  <p>Result: {{ result }}</p>
  <p>{{ operationMessage }}</p>
 </div>
</template>
```

2. **Script**: Define the data properties and methods for the calculator logic.

```javascript
<script>
export default {
  data() {
```

```
    return {
      number1: 0,
      number2: 0,
      operation: 'add', // Default operation
      result: 0,
      operationMessage: ''
    };
  },
  computed: {
    // Computed property to calculate the result
based on the operation
    result() {
      let res = 0;
      switch (this.operation) {
        case 'add':
          res = this.number1 + this.number2;
          break;
        case 'subtract':
          res = this.number1 - this.number2;
          break;
        case 'multiply':
          res = this.number1 * this.number2;
          break;
        case 'divide':
          if (this.number2 !== 0) {
            res = this.number1 / this.number2;
          } else {
            res = 'Error: Division by zero';
          }
```

```
        break;
    }
    return res;
  },
  operationMessage() {
    return    `You    are    performing    the
${this.operation} operation.`;
  }
 },
 watch: {
  // Watch for changes in the operation and
display a message when the operation changes
  operation(newOperation) {
    this.operationMessage = `You selected the
${newOperation} operation.`;
  }
 }
};
</script>
```

3. **Explanation**:

   o **Computed Property (result)**: This property computes the result of the operation based on the values of number1, number2, and the selected operation. It is recalculated only when the dependent data changes (i.e., when number1, number2, or operation changes).

- o **Watcher (`operation`)**: The watcher on `operation` listens for changes to the selected operation (add, subtract, multiply, divide). When the operation changes, it updates the `operationMessage` to reflect the new operation.
- o The `v-model` directive binds the input fields to `number1` and `number2`, allowing two-way data binding. The buttons allow the user to select the operation, which triggers a change in the `operation` data property.

4. **Result**:
   - o When the user inputs numbers and selects an operation, the result is computed and displayed automatically.
   - o The message also updates dynamically to show the current operation.

Summary:

In this chapter, we explored **computed properties** and **watchers** in Vue.js. Computed properties allow you to perform calculations or transformations based on data, while watchers let you react to changes in data and execute custom logic, such as side effects or asynchronous tasks.

We also built a real-world **calculator app** that demonstrated the power of computed properties and watchers. The calculator computes results based on user input and updates the operation message dynamically.

In the next chapter, we will explore **Vue Router**, which allows you to build multi-page applications and manage navigation between different views.

CHAPTER 9

VUE ROUTER: ADDING NAVIGATION TO YOUR APP

Introduction to Vue Router

Vue Router is the official routing library for Vue.js, and it enables you to build **single-page applications (SPAs)** by managing navigation between different views or pages without requiring a full page reload. In a single-page application, the application's view is updated dynamically based on the URL, and only the relevant part of the page is re-rendered, providing a smooth, fast user experience.

Vue Router helps you map URLs to components, handle navigation, and manage the state of your app. With Vue Router, you can:

- Define routes and associate them with components.
- Perform navigation between views.
- Use history mode or hash mode to manage the URL.
- Implement nested routes and dynamic routing.
- Handle programmatic navigation and route guards for more advanced routing behavior.

In Vue.js, the Vue Router library makes it easy to set up routes and manage navigation within the application. By using Vue Router, you can create multi-page applications that feel like traditional websites but with the performance and behavior of SPAs.

Setting Up Routes and Navigation

Setting up Vue Router in a Vue.js application requires the following basic steps:

1. Install Vue Router.
2. Create routes that map URLs to components.
3. Use the `<router-view>` element to display components for specific routes.
4. Use `<router-link>` to provide navigation links to users.

Installing Vue Router

To start using Vue Router, you need to install it via npm or yarn:

```
bash
```

```
npm install vue-router
```

After installing Vue Router, you need to import and configure it within your Vue application.

Setting Up Basic Routes

Once Vue Router is installed, you can define routes by mapping each route to a specific component. A route in Vue Router consists of a `path` (URL) and a `component` (the component to render when that URL is visited).

Example:

```javascript
// router.js
import Vue from 'vue';
import VueRouter from 'vue-router';
import Home from './components/Home.vue';
import About from './components/About.vue';

Vue.use(VueRouter);

const routes = [
  { path: '/', component: Home },
  { path: '/about', component: About }
];

const router = new VueRouter({
  routes // short for `routes: routes`
});

export default router;
```

Creating the Main Vue Instance

In your main `app.js` (or `main.js`) file, import Vue Router and the routes configuration, and then create the Vue instance with the router.

javascript

```
// main.js
import Vue from 'vue';
import App from './App.vue';
import router from './router';

new Vue({
    render: h => h(App),
    router // Inject the router into the Vue
instance
}).$mount('#app');
```

Using `<router-view>` and `<router-link>`

The `<router-view>` element is where the matched component will be rendered based on the current URL. Use `<router-link>` to create links for navigation.

Example:

html

```
<template>
```

```
<div>
  <nav>
    <router-link to="/">Home</router-link>
    <router-link    to="/about">About</router-
link>
  </nav>

    <router-view></router-view>    <!--    Render
matched component here -->
  </div>
</template>
```

In this example, clicking on the "Home" or "About" links will navigate to their respective routes (/ and /about), and the appropriate component will be rendered inside the <router-view>.

Dynamic Routing and Nested Routes

Vue Router also supports **dynamic routing** and **nested routes**, which are essential for building complex applications with multiple levels of navigation.

Dynamic Routing

Dynamic routing allows you to create routes that depend on parameters in the URL. For example, you can create routes where a part of the URL changes dynamically based on an ID or other data.

Example of dynamic routing:

```
javascript
```

```javascript
// router.js
import          UserProfile          from
'./components/UserProfile.vue';

const routes = [
  { path: '/user/:id', component: UserProfile }
// :id is a dynamic parameter
];
```

In this example, the `:id` is a dynamic parameter in the route path. When the user visits `/user/123`, the component `UserProfile` will be rendered, and the value of `id` (in this case, `123`) can be accessed within the `UserProfile` component.

```
javascript
```

```javascript
// UserProfile.vue
<template>
  <div>
    <h1>User Profile for {{ userId }}</h1>
  </div>
</template>

<script>
export default {
```

```
computed: {
  userId() {
    return this.$route.params.id;  // Access
the dynamic route parameter
  }
}
}
</script>
```

In this case, `this.$route.params.id` will give you the value
of the dynamic `id` parameter from the URL.

Nested Routes

Nested routes allow you to display components inside other
components, creating a hierarchical structure for your app.

Example of nested routes:

javascript

```
// router.js
import Home from './components/Home.vue';
import              Dashboard              from
'./components/Dashboard.vue';
import           UserProfile              from
'./components/UserProfile.vue';

const routes = [
  {
```

```
    path: '/',
    component: Home,
    children: [
      {
        path: 'dashboard',
        component: Dashboard,
        children: [
          {
            path: ':userId',
            component: UserProfile
          }
        ]
      }
    ]
  }
];
```

In this example:

- The Home component contains a <router-view> where the Dashboard component is rendered.
- The Dashboard component itself has a nested route for UserProfile where userId is a dynamic route parameter.

The <router-view> inside the Home component will display the Dashboard component, and the <router-view> inside the Dashboard component will display the UserProfile component.

html

```
<!-- Home.vue -->
<template>
  <div>
    <h1>Home Page</h1>
    <router-link     to="/dashboard">Go     to
Dashboard</router-link>
    <router-view></router-view>   <!--   Display
nested routes here -->
  </div>
</template>
```

This allows for a clean, nested structure, making it easy to organize your app's layout and views.

Real-World Example: Building a Multi-Page Application

Let's build a simple **multi-page application** that uses Vue Router. The app will have a home page, an about page, and a user profile page where the user's information is displayed based on their unique ID.

1. **Template**: Set up basic navigation using <router-link> and the <router-view> for displaying content.

html

```
<template>
```

```html
<div>
  <nav>
    <router-link to="/">Home</router-link>
    <router-link   to="/about">About</router-link>
    <router-link to="/user/1">User 1</router-link>
    <router-link to="/user/2">User 2</router-link>
  </nav>

  <router-view></router-view> <!-- This is where matched components will render -->
  </div>
</template>
```

2. **Router Setup**: Define routes for the home page, about page, and dynamic user profile page.

javascript

```javascript
// router.js
import Home from './components/Home.vue';
import About from './components/About.vue';
import UserProfile from './components/UserProfile.vue';

const routes = [
  { path: '/', component: Home },
  { path: '/about', component: About },
```

```
{ path: '/user/:id', component: UserProfile }
];
```

3. **UserProfile Component**: Display user information based on the dynamic route parameter.

javascript

```javascript
// UserProfile.vue
<template>
  <div>
    <h1>User Profile for {{ userId }}</h1>
    <p>Details about user {{ userId }}...</p>
  </div>
</template>

<script>
export default {
  computed: {
    userId() {
      return this.$route.params.id;  // Access
the dynamic 'id' parameter
    }
  }
};
</script>
```

4. **Main Application Setup**: Import Vue Router and set up the app to use it.

```
javascript

// main.js
import Vue from 'vue';
import App from './App.vue';
import VueRouter from 'vue-router';
import router from './router';

Vue.use(VueRouter);

new Vue({
  render: h => h(App),
  router
}).$mount('#app');
```

5. **Result**:

- o The user can navigate between the **Home** and **About** pages using the links.
- o The **User Profile** page will display user-specific information based on the dynamic id in the URL (e.g., /user/1 or /user/2).

This simple app demonstrates how to use **Vue Router** to create a multi-page application, handle dynamic routing, and organize your app with nested routes.

Summary:

In this chapter, we introduced **Vue Router** and explored how to set up routes and manage navigation within a Vue application. We learned how to:

- Set up routes and navigate between pages using `<router-link>` and `<router-view>`.
- Use **dynamic routing** to handle parameters in URLs.
- Implement **nested routes** to create complex layouts with hierarchical views.

Finally, we built a **multi-page application** that demonstrated Vue Router's capabilities in handling navigation and displaying different content based on the URL. In the next chapter, we will cover **Vue's form handling** and **validation techniques**, enabling you to work with user inputs in a more robust and interactive way.

CHAPTER 10

STATE MANAGEMENT WITH VUEX

What is State Management?

State management is a pattern used in software development to manage the state (or data) of an application in a centralized and predictable way. It ensures that the state is consistent across the entire application, making it easier to debug, scale, and maintain.

In modern JavaScript frameworks like Vue.js, the **state** typically refers to the data that drives the user interface. Managing the state across different components can become challenging, especially in large applications where different components need access to the same data.

Without a proper state management system, different components might manage their own state independently, leading to inconsistencies, difficult-to-maintain code, and challenges when data needs to be shared between multiple components.

Vuex is Vue's official state management library, which provides a centralized store for all the components in an application. It works by storing the state in a global object (the **store**) and allows

115

components to access, modify, and react to changes in the state in a consistent and predictable way.

Introduction to Vuex for State Management

Vuex is inspired by the Flux architecture, which emphasizes a unidirectional data flow. It works by providing a centralized **store** where the application's state is stored. Vuex allows you to:

- **Centralize state**: Manage all data in one place.
- **Use mutations**: Mutate the state in a predictable manner.
- **Actions**: Perform asynchronous operations like API calls before committing mutations.
- **Getters**: Retrieve and compute derived state from the store.

Vuex is especially useful in large applications where many components need to share state, as it helps maintain a clean, organized way to manage the data and reduce the complexity of the application.

Installing Vuex

To start using Vuex, you first need to install it:

```bash
```

```bash
npm install vuex
```

Then, you import Vuex and set it up in your Vue application:

```javascript

import Vue from 'vue';
import Vuex from 'vuex';


Vue.use(Vuex);

const store = new Vuex.Store({
  // state, mutations, actions, getters will be here
});
```

Store, Mutations, Actions, and Getters

In Vuex, you interact with the **store** to access and modify state, using the following concepts:

1. **State**: The source of truth. State holds the application's data and is stored in the Vuex store.
2. **Mutations**: Functions that modify the state in a synchronous manner.
3. **Actions**: Functions that can perform asynchronous operations before committing mutations.
4. **Getters**: Functions that compute derived state based on the state stored in Vuex. They can be thought of as computed properties for the store.

State

State is a simple object that contains the data your application needs. You define state in the Vuex store:

javascript

```
const store = new Vuex.Store({
  state: {
    counter: 0
  }
});
```

To access the state in a component, you use the $store object:

javascript

```
computed: {
  counter() {
    return this.$store.state.counter;
  }
}
```

Mutations

Mutations are responsible for modifying the state. They are synchronous functions that directly change the state. To modify the state, you need to commit a mutation using this.$store.commit():

```javascript

const store = new Vuex.Store({
  state: {
    counter: 0
  },
  mutations: {
    increment(state) {
      state.counter++;
    },
    decrement(state) {
      state.counter--;
    }
  }
});
```

In your component, you can commit a mutation to change the state:

```javascript

methods: {
  incrementCounter() {
    this.$store.commit('increment');
  },
  decrementCounter() {
    this.$store.commit('decrement');
  }
}
```

Actions

Actions are used to perform asynchronous operations (like fetching data or calling an API). Actions can commit mutations once the asynchronous operation is completed. Unlike mutations, actions are asynchronous and can use `async/await` or `Promise`.

```javascript
const store = new Vuex.Store({
  state: {
    counter: 0
  },
  mutations: {
    increment(state) {
      state.counter++;
    }
  },
  actions: {
    async incrementAsync({ commit }) {
      // Simulating an async operation (e.g., API call)
      await new Promise(resolve => setTimeout(resolve, 1000));
      commit('increment');
    }
  }
});
```

You can dispatch an action in your component using this.$store.dispatch():

javascript

```
methods: {
  incrementAsyncCounter() {
    this.$store.dispatch('incrementAsync');
  }
}
```

Getters

Getters are used to retrieve derived state. You can use getters to compute values based on the current state, just like Vue's computed properties, but they are specific to the Vuex store.

javascript

```
const store = new Vuex.Store({
  state: {
    counter: 0
  },
  getters: {
    doubledCounter(state) {
      return state.counter * 2;
    }
  }
});
```

You can access getters in your component using this.$store.getters:

javascript

```
computed: {
  doubledCounter() {
    return this.$store.getters.doubledCounter;
  }
}
```

Real-World Example: Building a Shopping Cart

Now, let's build a **shopping cart** example where we can add items, remove them, and update the quantity. This will demonstrate how to use **Vuex** for state management.

1. **Template**: Create a simple shopping cart with buttons for adding and removing items.

html

```
<template>
  <div>
    <h1>Shopping Cart</h1>
    <div>
      <button      @click="addItem('Apple')">Add
Apple</button>
      <button      @click="addItem('Banana')">Add
Banana</button>
```

```
    </div>

    <ul>
      <li  v-for="(quantity,    item)   in   cart"
:key="item">
        {{ item }} - Quantity: {{ quantity }}
        <button
@click="removeItem(item)">Remove</button>
      </li>
    </ul>
    <p>Total Items: {{ totalItems }}</p>
  </div>
</template>
```

2. **Script**: Define the state, mutations, actions, and getters for the shopping cart.

```
javascript
```

```javascript
<script>
import { mapState, mapGetters, mapActions } from
'vuex';

export default {
  computed: {
    ...mapState(['cart']),
    ...mapGetters(['totalItems'])
  },
  methods: {
    ...mapActions(['addItem', 'removeItem'])
```

```
    }
};
</script>
```

3. **Vuex Store**: Define the state, mutations, actions, and getters in the Vuex store.

```javascript
import Vue from 'vue';
import Vuex from 'vuex';

Vue.use(Vuex);

export const store = new Vuex.Store({
  state: {
    cart: {}
  },
  mutations: {
    addToCart(state, item) {
      if (state.cart[item]) {
        state.cart[item]++;
      } else {
        state.cart[item] = 1;
      }
    },
    removeFromCart(state, item) {
      if (state.cart[item]) {
        state.cart[item]--;
        if (state.cart[item] === 0) {
```

```
        delete state.cart[item];
    }
  }
}
},
actions: {
  addItem({ commit }, item) {
    commit('addToCart', item);
  },
  removeItem({ commit }, item) {
    commit('removeFromCart', item);
  }
},
getters: {
  totalItems(state) {
    return
Object.values(state.cart).reduce((sum, quantity)
=> sum + quantity, 0);
  }
}
});
```

4. **Explanation**:

   o The **state** holds the `cart` object, which is a dictionary of items and their quantities.

   o **Mutations** modify the state by adding or removing items from the cart.

- o **Actions** dispatch mutations to modify the state asynchronously (although in this simple case, actions are synchronous).
- o **Getters** calculate the total number of items in the cart by summing the quantities of all items.

5. **Result**:
   - o You can add items to the cart by clicking the "Add Apple" or "Add Banana" buttons.
   - o The cart updates dynamically, showing the current quantity of each item.
   - o You can remove items from the cart, and the quantity decreases or the item is removed entirely when the quantity reaches 0.

Summary:

In this chapter, we explored **Vuex** and how it helps manage state in a Vue.js application. We covered the fundamental concepts of **state**, **mutations**, **actions**, and **getters**, and how they work together to manage and access the application state in a predictable way.

We also built a **shopping cart** example that demonstrated how to add, remove, and update items in a centralized store using Vuex.

In the next chapter, we will cover **Vue's lifecycle hooks**, how they work in conjunction with Vuex, and how to handle complex workflows in your application.

CHAPTER 11

FORMS AND VALIDATION IN VUE

Handling Forms in Vue.js

Forms are a common feature in most web applications, allowing users to submit data. In Vue.js, handling forms is simple and intuitive, thanks to its two-way data binding system. With Vue, you can bind form inputs to the component's data, automatically updating the data when the user interacts with the form fields.

To handle forms in Vue.js, you typically use the `v-model` directive, which provides two-way data binding for form elements. This allows changes made in the form to be reflected in the data and vice versa, ensuring your data stays synchronized with the UI.

Basic Form Handling in Vue

Here's an example of a simple form with input fields bound to Vue data using `v-model`:

html

```
<template>
```

```
<div>
  <h1>User Registration</h1>
  <form @submit.prevent="handleSubmit">
    <div>
      <label for="username">Username:</label>
      <input  type="text"  v-model="username"
id="username" required>
    </div>

    <div>
      <label for="email">Email:</label>
      <input   type="email"   v-model="email"
id="email" required>
    </div>

    <div>
      <label for="password">Password:</label>
      <input        type="password"        v-
model="password" id="password" required>
    </div>

    <button type="submit">Register</button>
  </form>
</div>
</template>

<script>
export default {
  data() {
```

```
return {
  username: '',
  email: '',
  password: ''
};
},
methods: {
  handleSubmit() {
    console.log("User     data     submitted:",
this.username, this.email, this.password);
    // You can handle the form submission logic
here, like sending the data to an API
  }
}
};
</script>
```

In this example:

- The v-model directive binds each form input to the corresponding data property (username, email, and password).
- The @submit.prevent="handleSubmit" ensures that when the form is submitted, it doesn't refresh the page and instead calls the handleSubmit method.
- The method handleSubmit logs the data to the console, but you can extend it to handle form submission, such as sending the data to a server.

Input Validation and Error Handling

Validating user input is an essential part of form handling. Vue provides several ways to handle validation, both with custom logic and with the help of third-party libraries.

Basic Input Validation

In Vue, you can perform simple validation in your methods or computed properties. For example, you can check whether the input meets certain criteria (e.g., required fields, valid email format, password strength).

Example of basic validation for the registration form:

javascript

```javascript
methods: {
  handleSubmit() {
    if (!this.username || !this.email ||
!this.password) {
      alert("All fields are required.");
      return;
    }
    if (!this.isValidEmail(this.email)) {
      alert("Please enter a valid email
address.");
      return;
    }
```

```
    console.log("Form submitted successfully:",
this.username, this.email, this.password);
  },
  isValidEmail(email) {
    const emailPattern = /^[a-zA-Z0-9._-]+@[a-
zA-Z0-9.-]+\.[a-zA-Z]{2,6}$/;
    return emailPattern.test(email);
  }
}
```

In this example:

- The `handleSubmit` method checks whether all fields are filled. If any of the fields are empty, it displays an error message.
- The `isValidEmail` method uses a regular expression to check if the email entered is in a valid format. If the email is invalid, an error message is shown.

Displaying Error Messages

You can display error messages to users based on validation checks. This can be done using Vue's reactive data and conditional rendering.

html

```
<template>
  <div>
```

```
<form @submit.prevent="handleSubmit">
  <div>
    <label for="username">Username:</label>
    <input   type="text"   v-model="username"
id="username" required>
    <p              v-if="errors.username"
class="error">{{ errors.username }}</p>
  </div>

  <div>
    <label for="email">Email:</label>
    <input   type="email"   v-model="email"
id="email" required>
    <p v-if="errors.email" class="error">{{
errors.email }}</p>
  </div>

  <div>
    <label for="password">Password:</label>
    <input         type="password"         v-
model="password" id="password" required>
    <p              v-if="errors.password"
class="error">{{ errors.password }}</p>
  </div>

  <button type="submit">Register</button>
</form>
  </div>
</template>
```

```
<script>
export default {
  data() {
    return {
      username: '',
      email: '',
      password: '',
      errors: {} // Object to store error
messages
    };
  },
  methods: {
    handleSubmit() {
      this.errors = {}; // Reset errors on submit
attempt
      let valid = true;

      if (!this.username) {
        this.errors.username = "Username is
required.";
        valid = false;
      }
      if              (!this.email           ||
!this.isValidEmail(this.email)) {
        this.errors.email = "Please enter a valid
email address.";
        valid = false;
      }
```

```
      if (!this.password) {
        this.errors.password  =  "Password  is
required.";
        valid = false;
      }

      if (valid) {
        console.log("Form              submitted
successfully:",    this.username,    this.email,
this.password);
      }
    },
    isValidEmail(email) {
      const emailPattern = /^[a-zA-Z0-9._-]+@[a-
zA-Z0-9.-]+\.[a-zA-Z]{2,6}$/;
      return emailPattern.test(email);
    }
  }
};
</script>

<style scoped>
.error {
  color: red;
}
}
</style>
```

In this example:

- The `errors` object stores error messages for each form field.
- The error messages are displayed below the respective input fields using `v-if` directives.
- If a form field is invalid, the corresponding error message is shown, and the form will not submit until all fields are valid.

Using Vue Form Libraries

For more complex forms and validation logic, you can use third-party libraries that integrate with Vue.js. Some popular libraries for form handling and validation in Vue include:

- **VeeValidate**: A powerful library for form validation in Vue, supporting both synchronous and asynchronous validation.
- **Vuelidate**: A lightweight library for handling validation in Vue.js, offering a flexible and simple API.
- **Vue Formulate**: A library for creating forms in Vue with built-in validation, custom inputs, and more.

Example with VeeValidate

Here's a simple example of how you might use **VeeValidate** for form validation in Vue.js:

1. Install VeeValidate:

```bash
bash

npm install vee-validate
```

2. Example form with validation:

```html
html

<template>
  <div>
    <h1>User Registration</h1>
    <form @submit.prevent="handleSubmit">
      <div>
        <label for="username">Username:</label>
        <input type="text" v-model="username"
name="username" v-validate="'required'" />
        <span v-if="errors.has('username')"
class="error">{{        errors.first('username')
}}</span>
      </div>

      <div>
        <label for="email">Email:</label>
        <input type="email" v-model="email"
name="email" v-validate="'required|email'" />
        <span v-if="errors.has('email')"
class="error">{{ errors.first('email') }}</span>
      </div>

      <div>
```

```
        <label for="password">Password:</label>
        <input         type="password"          v-
model="password"          name="password"          v-
validate="'required|min:6'" />
        <span         v-if="errors.has('password')"
class="error">{{         errors.first('password')
}}</span>
      </div>

      <button type="submit">Register</button>
    </form>
  </div>
</template>

<script>
import { ValidationProvider, extend } from 'vee-
validate';
import { required, email, min } from 'vee-
validate/dist/rules';

// Add VeeValidate rules
extend('required', required);
extend('email', email);
extend('min', min);

export default {
  data() {
    return {
      username: '',
```

```
      email: '',
      password: ''
    };
  },
  methods: {
    handleSubmit() {
      console.log('Form            submitted:',
this.username, this.email, this.password);
    }
  }
};
</script>

<style scoped>
.error {
  color: red;
}
</style>
```

In this example:

- **VeeValidate** is used to add validation rules to each form field.
- The `v-validate` directive is used to specify the validation rules for each field (e.g., `required`, `email`, `min:6`).
- Error messages are displayed below the form fields if validation fails.

Real-World Example: User Registration and Login

Building on the concepts above, we can create a real-world user registration and login form with Vue.js. The form will include validation and error handling, allowing users to enter their credentials, submit the form, and receive feedback.

The registration form will have the following features:

- Input validation (username, email, password)
- Display error messages if the fields are invalid
- Success message upon successful registration or login attempt

Summary:

In this chapter, we explored **form handling** in Vue.js, focusing on:

- How to bind form fields to Vue data using the `v-model` directive.
- How to implement basic **input validation** and error handling in Vue using custom methods and conditional rendering.
- How to use third-party libraries like **VeeValidate** for more complex validation scenarios.

Finally, we built a **user registration form** with input validation and error handling to ensure the form data is valid before submission. In the next chapter, we will explore **Vue Router** in detail, allowing us to manage navigation between different views in our application.

CHAPTER 12

WORKING WITH APIS IN VUE.JS

Making HTTP Requests with Axios

In modern web applications, interacting with external services or databases is a common task. In Vue.js, the most popular way to make HTTP requests is by using a library like **Axios**. Axios is a promise-based HTTP client that makes it easy to send requests to a server and handle responses.

Installing Axios

To start using Axios in your Vue.js project, you need to install it. If you haven't already installed Axios, you can do so via npm:

bash

```
npm install axios
```

Once installed, you can import Axios into your Vue components or services:

javascript

```
import axios from 'axios';
```

Making a Simple GET Request

A basic GET request with Axios fetches data from an external API. Here's an example of how to fetch data from an API when the component is created.

```javascript
```

```
<template>
  <div>
    <h1>Data from API</h1>
    <ul>
      <li        v-for="item         in        items"
:key="item.id">{{ item.name }}</li>
    </ul>
  </div>
</template>

<script>
import axios from 'axios';

export default {
  data() {
    return {
      items: [] // Array to hold the fetched data
    };
  },
  created() {
```

```
// Make the GET request when the component is
created
  axios.get('https://api.example.com/items')
    .then(response => {
      this.items = response.data; // Store the
fetched data in the items array
    })
    .catch(error => {
      console.error("There    was    an    error
fetching the data:", error);
    });
  }
};
</script>
```

In this example:

- The `axios.get()` method makes a GET request to the specified URL.
- When the request is successful, the data is saved to the `items` array.
- If the request fails, an error message is logged to the console.

Making a POST Request

To send data to a server (for example, creating a new resource), you can use the `axios.post()` method.

144

Example of making a POST request to send user data:

javascript

```
<template>
  <div>
    <h1>Create User</h1>
    <form @submit.prevent="createUser">
      <input v-model="name" placeholder="Enter name">
      <input v-model="email" placeholder="Enter email">
      <button type="submit">Submit</button>
    </form>
  </div>
</template>

<script>
import axios from 'axios';

export default {
  data() {
    return {
      name: '',
      email: ''
    };
  },
  methods: {
    createUser() {
      const userData = {
```

145

```
      name: this.name,
      email: this.email
    };


axios.post('https://api.example.com/users',
userData)
        .then(response => {
          console.log('User              created:',
response.data);
        })
        .catch(error => {
          console.error('There    was    an    error
creating the user:', error);
        });
    }
  }
};
</script>
```

In this example:

- The `createUser` method collects the data from the form
  fields and sends a POST request with the user data.
- The `axios.post()` method is used to send data to the
  API endpoint (`https://api.example.com/users`).

Handling API Responses in Vue

Handling responses from an API is an essential part of working with APIs. Once a request is made using Axios, you will typically handle the **response data** and **errors**.

Handling Successful Responses

When the request is successful, the response data is returned in the `.then()` block of the promise. You can access the data through `response.data`.

Example:

```javascript
axios.get('https://api.example.com/items')
  .then(response => {
    console.log('API Response:', response.data);
    this.items = response.data; // Store the data
in the component's state
  })
  .catch(error => {
    console.error("Error     fetching     data:",
error);
  });
```

Here, `response.data` contains the actual data returned from the API, and you can then store it in the component's data properties.

Handling Errors

If the request fails, Axios will return an error, and you can handle it in the `.catch()` block. You can use the error object to log the error, show a message to the user, or perform other actions like retrying the request.

```javascript
axios.get('https://api.example.com/items')
  .then(response => {
    this.items = response.data;
  })
  .catch(error => {
    console.error("Error              occurred:",
error.response);
    this.errorMessage = 'An error occurred while
fetching the data';
  });
```

In this example:

- The error object provides detailed information about what went wrong (e.g., network error, server error, etc.).
- You can display an error message to the user if necessary.

Real-World Example: Fetching Data from an External API

Let's build a real-world example where we fetch and display data from an external API. In this example, we'll fetch a list of users from a mock API and display them in a list.

1. **Template**: Create a simple list to display fetched user data.

html

```
<template>
  <div>
    <h1>User List</h1>
    <div v-if="loading">Loading...</div>
    <div v-if="errorMessage" class="error">{{
errorMessage }}</div>

    <ul v-if="!loading && !errorMessage">
      <li v-for="user in users"
:key="user.id">{{ user.name }} - {{ user.email
}}</li>
    </ul>
  </div>
</template>
```

2. **Script**: Define the data and methods for making the API request.

149

javascript

```
<script>
import axios from 'axios';

export default {
  data() {
    return {
      users: [], // Array to store user data
      loading: true, // Boolean to track loading
state
      errorMessage: null // String to store error
message
    };
  },
  created() {
    this.fetchUsers();
  },
  methods: {
    fetchUsers() {

axios.get('https://jsonplaceholder.typicode.com
/users')
      .then(response => {
        this.users = response.data; // Store
the fetched user data
        this.loading = false; // Set loading to
false once data is fetched
      })
```

```
.catch(error => {
    this.errorMessage = 'Failed to fetch
users. Please try again later.'; // Set error
message
    this.loading = false; // Set loading to
false even on error
    });
  }
 }
};
</script>
```

3. **Explanation**:

   o **axios.get('https://jsonplaceholder. typicode.com/users')**: Fetches user data from the mock API.

   o **this.users**: Stores the fetched data in the users array.

   o **loading**: A boolean that displays a "Loading..." message while data is being fetched.

   o **errorMessage**: If the request fails, this variable stores the error message, which is displayed to the user.

4. **Result**:

   o The app initially shows a "Loading..." message while the data is being fetched.

   o If the request is successful, the user list is displayed.

o   If there is an error, an error message is displayed.

Summary:

In this chapter, we explored **working with APIs in Vue.js** using Axios, a popular HTTP client. We covered:

- How to **make HTTP requests** using Axios (GET, POST, etc.).
- How to **handle API responses** and display data in your Vue components.
- How to manage **loading states** and **error handling**.
- We built a real-world **user list** application that fetched data from an external API and displayed it.

With Axios, handling asynchronous data fetching becomes straightforward, and Vue's reactive data system ensures that the UI updates automatically when the data changes. In the next chapter, we will dive into **Vuex** for state management, which can help manage the global state of your application when working with complex data.

CHAPTER 13

VUE.JS TRANSITIONS AND ANIMATIONS

Introduction to Vue.js Transitions

In Vue.js, **transitions** and **animations** make it easy to add smooth and interactive visual effects when elements enter or leave the DOM. Whether you're animating elements on page load, when data changes, or during state transitions, Vue provides a powerful system to manage these effects in a simple and declarative way.

Vue's transition system is built around the idea of wrapping an element or component in a `<transition>` wrapper and applying custom animations or transition effects when the element is added, removed, or updated.

Vue allows you to add transitions in several scenarios:

1. **Entering**: When an element is inserted into the DOM.
2. **Leaving**: When an element is removed from the DOM.
3. **List transitions**: When items are added or removed from lists dynamically.

Using CSS and JavaScript Animations in Vue

Vue supports both **CSS-based transitions** and **JavaScript-based animations**. You can use CSS classes or inline styles to control animations, or you can use JavaScript for more complex scenarios that require control over the animation timeline.

CSS Transitions in Vue.js

CSS transitions allow you to define changes to an element's style over a specified duration. Vue makes it simple to add transitions to DOM elements with minimal code.

1. **Basic CSS Transition**: To animate an element's transition (e.g., opacity, height, color), you can use Vue's `<transition>` wrapper with CSS classes.

Example:

html

```
<template>
  <div>
    <button          @click="show          =
!show">Toggle</button>
    <transition name="fade">
      <p    v-if="show">This    is    a    fading
paragraph.</p>
    </transition>
```

154

```
  </div>
</template>

<script>
export default {
  data() {
    return {
      show: false
    };
  }
};
</script>

<style>
.fade-enter-active, .fade-leave-active {
  transition: opacity 1s;
}
.fade-enter, .fade-leave-to {
  opacity: 0;
}
</style>
```

In this example:

- The `v-if="show"` directive conditionally renders the paragraph element.
- The `<transition>` wrapper applies the `fade` transition.
- When the element enters or leaves, Vue applies the specified CSS classes (fade-enter-active, fade-

155

leave-active, etc.), which control the animation duration and effect.

The fade-enter-active and fade-leave-active classes control the transition's duration and easing, while the fade-enter and fade-leave-to classes define the initial and final states of the element.

JavaScript Transitions in Vue.js

JavaScript transitions provide more control over the timing, flow, and behavior of animations. When you need to use JavaScript to trigger an animation (e.g., when you need to animate properties that aren't easily animated with CSS), you can use Vue's **transition hooks**.

Example of a JavaScript transition using before-enter, enter, and leave hooks:

html

```
<template>
  <div>
    <button            @click="show      =
!show">Toggle</button>
    <transition       @before-enter="beforeEnter"
@enter="enter" @leave="leave">
```

```
    <p    v-if="show">This    is    a    sliding
paragraph.</p>
  </transition>
 </div>
</template>

<script>
export default {
  data() {
    return {
      show: false
    };
  },
  methods: {
    beforeEnter(el) {
      el.style.transform = 'translateX(100%)';
      el.style.transition = 'transform 1s';
    },
    enter(el, done) {
      el.offsetHeight; // trigger reflow
      el.style.transform = 'translateX(0)';
      done();
    },
    leave(el, done) {
      el.style.transform = 'translateX(100%)';
      done();
    }
  }
};
```

```
</script>
```

In this example:

- The `before-enter` hook prepares the element for the transition, setting its initial position (`translateX(100%)`).
- The `enter` hook animates the element into place by changing its `transform` property.
- The `leave` hook slides the element out by animating it back to `translateX(100%)`.
- The `done()` function is called to let Vue know the transition has finished.

This approach gives you complete control over the transition process and is especially useful for complex animations that involve multiple properties or when you want to trigger actions after the animation completes.

Practical Example: Animating List Items and Elements

Let's build a real-world example where we animate the addition and removal of list items using Vue.js transitions. We will use both **CSS** and **JavaScript** to animate the items as they enter and leave the DOM.

Step-by-Step Example

1. **Template**: Create a list of items that can be added and removed with buttons.

html

```html
<template>
  <div>
    <h1>Animated List</h1>
    <button @click="addItem">Add Item</button>
    <button                 @click="removeItem"
:disabled="!items.length">Remove Item</button>

    <transition-group name="list-fade" tag="ul">
      <li   v-for="(item,   index)   in   items"
:key="item.id" class="list-item">
        {{ item.name }}
      </li>
    </transition-group>
  </div>
</template>
```

2. **Script**: Define the data and methods for adding and removing items from the list.

javascript

```javascript
<script>
export default {
```

```
data() {
  return {
    items: [] // Array to store the list items
  };
},
methods: {
  addItem() {
    const newItem = {
      id: Date.now(),
      name: `Item ${this.items.length + 1}`
    };
    this.items.push(newItem);
  },
  removeItem() {
    this.items.pop();
  }
}
};
</script>
```

3. **Styles**: Add CSS transitions to animate the list items as they enter and leave the DOM.

css

```
<style scoped>
.list-fade-enter-active, .list-fade-leave-active
{
  transition: opacity 1s, transform 0.5s;
}
```

```
.list-fade-enter, .list-fade-leave-to {
  opacity: 0;
  transform: translateY(20px);
}


.list-item {
  padding: 10px;
  margin: 5px;
  background-color: #f9f9f9;
  border: 1px solid #ddd;
  border-radius: 5px;
}
</style>
```

4. **Explanation**:

- o We are using Vue's **transition-group** to animate a list of items. The `tag="ul"` tells Vue to render a `<ul>` element around the list of `<li>` items.

- o **v-for="(item, index) in items"** iterates through the `items` array and renders each item in the list.

- o The **transition-group** wrapper applies the `list-fade` transition to all items, and Vue automatically animates the entering and leaving of list items based on the CSS classes.

161

- o The `.list-fade-enter-active` and `.list-fade-leave-active` classes define the transition's duration and easing.
- o The `.list-fade-enter` and `.list-fade-leave-to` classes define the initial and final states of the items as they fade in and out, with a slight upward movement (using `translateY`).

5. **Result**:
   - o Clicking "Add Item" adds a new item to the list with a smooth fade-in and slide-up effect.
   - o Clicking "Remove Item" removes the last item in the list with a fade-out and slide-down effect.

Summary:

In this chapter, we explored **Vue.js transitions and animations**, focusing on:

- The basic concept of **transitions** and how to apply them using the `<transition>` wrapper.
- How to use **CSS-based transitions** to animate elements entering and leaving the DOM.
- How to create more complex animations using **JavaScript hooks** to control animations with more precision.

- We also built a **dynamic list example** where items are added and removed with smooth animations, demonstrating the power of Vue's transition system.

In the next chapter, we will explore **Vuex**, a state management library for Vue.js that helps you manage and centralize your app's state in a predictable way, especially useful for larger applications with complex data management needs.

CHAPTER 14

TESTING VUE.JS APPLICATIONS

Introduction to Testing in Vue.js

Testing is a crucial part of software development, ensuring that the application behaves as expected, performs well, and does not break with new changes. In Vue.js, testing typically involves **unit testing** individual components and **integration testing** to ensure the entire system works together as expected.

Testing Vue.js applications can be done with various tools, but the most common approach is to use **Jest** for JavaScript testing combined with **Vue Test Utils** for interacting with Vue components in a test environment. Vue Test Utils is the official utility library for testing Vue components, providing useful methods to mount, render, and interact with components in an isolated environment.

In this chapter, we will cover:

- The basics of testing in Vue.js applications.
- How to write **unit tests** for Vue components.
- Using **Jest** with Vue to run and manage tests.
- A real-world example of writing tests for Vue components.

Unit Testing Vue Components

Unit tests are focused on testing individual components in isolation. For Vue components, unit tests can verify that the component:

1. Renders correctly with different input values.
2. Emits events when needed.
3. Interacts with data correctly.
4. Performs logic inside methods correctly.

Vue Test Utils: The Official Library for Vue Testing

Vue Test Utils is the official testing utility library for Vue.js that makes it easy to test Vue components. It provides APIs to:

- Mount components.
- Simulate events.
- Access component data, methods, and computed properties.
- Verify component rendering.

Setting Up Jest with Vue

Jest is a popular testing framework for JavaScript that works well with Vue.js. To get started, you need to install Jest along with Vue Test Utils.

1. **Install Dependencies:**

bash

```bash
npm install --save-dev jest vue-test-utils @vue/test-utils babel-jest
```

2. **Configure Jest:** In your `package.json`, add a `test` script and Jest configuration to set up Vue-specific testing:

json

```json
"scripts": {
  "test": "jest"
},
"jest": {
  "transform": {
    "^.+\\.vue$": "vue-jest",
    "^.+\\.js$": "babel-jest"
  },
  "moduleFileExtensions": [
    "js",
    "vue",
    "json"
  ]
}
```

166

3. **Create a Jest Test File:** Your test files should be placed in the `__tests__` directory, or you can create them alongside your component files. Test files typically end in `.spec.js` or `.test.js`.

Writing a Simple Unit Test

Let's write a simple unit test for a Vue component that displays a message passed via a prop.

javascript

```
// Message.vue
<template>
  <div>
    <p>{{ message }}</p>
  </div>
</template>

<script>
export default {
  props: {
    message: String
  }
};
</script>
```

Now, let's write a unit test for the `Message` component.

```javascript
// Message.spec.js
import { mount } from '@vue/test-utils';
import Message from '@/components/Message.vue';

describe('Message.vue', () => {
  it('renders props.message when passed', () =>
{
    const message = 'Hello, world!';
    const wrapper = mount(Message, {
      propsData: { message }
    });

    // Assert that the component renders the
correct message
    expect(wrapper.text()).toContain(message);
  });
});
```

Explanation:

- We use `mount()` from **Vue Test Utils** to mount the component in the test.
- We pass a prop (`message`) to the component using the `propsData` option.
- We then assert that the component's rendered text contains the message passed as a prop using Jest's `expect()` and `toContain()`.

Using Jest with Vue

Jest is a popular testing framework for JavaScript, and it works seamlessly with Vue. When testing Vue components, Jest allows you to:

- Run tests asynchronously.
- Mock modules and functions.
- Use snapshots to test component rendering.
- Handle setup and teardown logic for each test.

Testing Methods and Events

Let's test a Vue component that has methods and emits events. Here's an example:

vue

```vue
<!-- Counter.vue -->
<template>
  <div>
    <p>{{ count }}</p>
    <button
@click="increment">Increment</button>
  </div>
</template>

<script>
export default {
```

```
data() {
  return {
    count: 0
  };
},
methods: {
  increment() {
    this.count++;
    this.$emit('incremented', this.count); //
Emit an event when incrementing
  }
}
};
</script>
```

Now, let's write a test for the Counter component:

javascript

```
// Counter.spec.js
import { mount } from '@vue/test-utils';
import Counter from '@/components/Counter.vue';

describe('Counter.vue', () => {
  it('increments the count when the button is
clicked', async () => {
    const wrapper = mount(Counter);

    // Simulate a click on the button
```

```
    await
wrapper.find('button').trigger('click');


    // Assert that the count has been incremented
    expect(wrapper.text()).toContain('1');
  });


  it('emits an incremented event when the button
is clicked', async () => {
    const wrapper = mount(Counter);

    // Simulate a click on the button
    await
wrapper.find('button').trigger('click');


    // Assert that the "incremented" event was
emitted with the correct payload

expect(wrapper.emitted().incremented[0]).toEqua
l([1]);
  });
});
```

Explanation:

- The first test checks if the count updates when the button
  is clicked.

- The second test checks that the component emits the `incremented` event with the correct payload (the new count value).

- We use `await wrapper.find('button').trigger('click')` to simulate a button click, ensuring that the method executes asynchronously.

Real-World Example: Writing Tests for Your Components

Let's look at a more practical example. We'll write tests for a **User Login Form** that includes form validation.

1. **Template:**

vue

```
<!-- LoginForm.vue -->
<template>
  <div>
    <form @submit.prevent="submitForm">
      <label for="email">Email</label>
      <input v-model="email" id="email"
type="email" required />
      <span v-if="emailError">Invalid email
address.</span>

      <label for="password">Password</label>
```

```
      <input  v-model="password"  id="password"
type="password" required />
      <span  v-if="passwordError">Password  must
be at least 6 characters long.</span>

      <button type="submit">Login</button>
    </form>
  </div>
</template>

<script>
export default {
  data() {
    return {
      email: '',
      password: '',
      emailError: false,
      passwordError: false
    };
  },
  methods: {
    submitForm() {
      this.emailError                        =
!this.validateEmail(this.email);
      this.passwordError                     =
!this.validatePassword(this.password);

      if              (!this.emailError       &&
!this.passwordError) {
```

173

```
      // Submit the form (e.g., make an API
call)
      this.$emit('login-success');
    }
  },
  validateEmail(email) {
    return       /^[a-zA-Z0-9._-]+@[a-zA-Z0-9.-
]+\.[a-zA-Z]{2,6}$/.test(email);
  },
  validatePassword(password) {
    return password.length >= 6;
  }
  }
};
</script>
```

2. **Test:**

```javascript
// LoginForm.spec.js
import { mount } from '@vue/test-utils';
import          LoginForm          from
'@/components/LoginForm.vue';

describe('LoginForm.vue', () => {
  it('shows email error if the email is invalid',
async () => {
    const wrapper = mount(LoginForm);
```

```
    // Set an invalid email
    await wrapper.setData({ email: 'invalid-
email' });

    // Trigger form submission
    await
wrapper.find('form').trigger('submit.prevent');

    // Check that the email error is displayed
    expect(wrapper.text()).toContain('Invalid
email address.');
  });

  it('shows password error if the password is too
short', async () => {
    const wrapper = mount(LoginForm);

    // Set a short password
    await wrapper.setData({ password: '12345'
});

    // Trigger form submission
    await
wrapper.find('form').trigger('submit.prevent');

    // Check that the password error is displayed
    expect(wrapper.text()).toContain('Password
must be at least 6 characters long.');
  });
```

```
it('emits login-success event if the form is
valid', async () => {
    const wrapper = mount(LoginForm);

    // Set valid email and password
    await          wrapper.setData({        email:
'test@example.com', password: 'password123' });

    // Trigger form submission
    await
wrapper.find('form').trigger('submit.prevent');

    // Assert that the login-success event was
emitted
    expect(wrapper.emitted().login-
success).toBeTruthy();
  });
});
```

Explanation:

- The first test checks if an error message is displayed when an invalid email is entered.
- The second test ensures that an error message appears when the password is too short.
- The third test simulates submitting the form with valid data and checks that the `login-success` event is emitted.

Summary:

In this chapter, we covered the fundamentals of **testing Vue.js applications**:

- We explored **unit testing** for Vue components using **Jest** and **Vue Test Utils**.
- We learned how to write tests for Vue components, including handling form validation, simulating events, and checking component behavior.
- We also demonstrated testing a **real-world login form** with form validation and custom events.

In the next chapter, we will delve into **Vuex**, which provides a centralized store for state management, making it easier to manage data across components in larger Vue applications.

CHAPTER 15

BEST PRACTICES FOR VUE.JS DEVELOPMENT

Introduction

Vue.js is an efficient and flexible framework for building interactive user interfaces. However, as with any framework, following best practices ensures that your Vue.js application is maintainable, scalable, and performant. In this chapter, we will cover best practices for organizing your Vue project, promoting code reusability, managing component communication, and optimizing performance.

Organizing Your Vue Project Structure

Organizing your project structure is crucial to keeping your codebase clean, manageable, and scalable. A well-structured project allows you and your team to work efficiently and understand the application at a glance. Vue does not enforce a specific structure, so it's up to the developer to decide on the organization.

Suggested Directory Structure

Here's a common directory structure for a large-scale Vue.js application:

bash

```
src/
  assets/            # Static assets (images,
fonts, etc.)
  components/        # Reusable Vue components
  views/            # Vue components corresponding
to routes (pages)
  router/           # Vue Router configuration
  store/            # Vuex store (state management)
  services/          # API service logic
  utils/            # Utility functions or mixins
  App.vue           # Root component
  main.js            # Main entry point for Vue
application
```

- **assets/**: Store all static files such as images, stylesheets, and fonts.
- **components/**: Keep reusable, smaller components that are not tied to a specific page.
- **views/**: Keep page-level components that are tied to specific routes (i.e., the views rendered by Vue Router).
- **router/**: Contains your routing configuration. This includes setting up routes for different views of your app.

179

- **store/**: Houses your Vuex store configuration to manage application state.
- **services/**: Centralized API calls or business logic.

Avoiding a "Flat" Structure

As your app grows, avoid placing all your components and assets in a single directory. Instead, group components by feature or section of your application. This improves maintainability and reduces confusion.

For example, instead of a flat structure:

css

```
components/
    Button.vue
    Input.vue
    Header.vue
    Footer.vue
```

Consider grouping related components:

css

```
components/
    layout/
        Header.vue
        Footer.vue
```

```
form/
  Button.vue
  Input.vue
```

Code Reusability and Modularization

One of the key principles of efficient development is maximizing code **reusability** and **modularization**. This ensures that components and code are easy to maintain and extend. Here are some strategies to improve code reuse in Vue.js:

Reusable Components

Make components **small and focused**. Each component should ideally serve a single purpose. If a component can be reused in multiple parts of your application, it should be made as generic and flexible as possible. For example:

vue

```vue
<!-- Button.vue -->
<template>
  <button    :class="['btn',    size,    color]"
@click="handleClick">
    <slot></slot>
  </button>
</template>

<script>
export default {
```

```
  props: {
    size: {
      type: String,
      default: 'medium'
    },
    color: {
      type: String,
      default: 'primary'
    }
  },
  methods: {
    handleClick() {
      this.$emit('click');
    }
  }
};
</script>

<style scoped>
.btn {
  padding: 10px 20px;
  border: none;
  cursor: pointer;
}

.medium {
  font-size: 14px;
}
```

```
.primary {
  background-color: blue;
  color: white;
}
</style>
```

In this example, the `Button` component is reusable, customizable by passing `size` and `color` props, and can be used throughout the app without having to duplicate code for each button.

Use Mixins for Shared Functionality

For shared methods or behavior, use **mixins**. A mixin is a way to encapsulate reusable logic that can be shared across components.

```javascript
// formMixin.js
export const formMixin = {
  data() {
    return {
      formData: {}
    };
  },
  methods: {
    resetForm() {
      this.formData = {};
    },
    validateForm() {
```

```
    // Add validation logic
    return true;
  }
 }
};
```

You can then include the mixin in any component:

javascript

```
import { formMixin } from '@/mixins/formMixin';

export default {
  mixins: [formMixin],
  methods: {
    submitForm() {
      if (this.validateForm()) {
        // Form submission logic
      }
    }
  }
};
```

Use Vuex for Shared State

When you need to manage state that needs to be accessed by multiple components, consider using **Vuex**. Vuex is a state management pattern and library for Vue.js that helps manage shared state across all components of your app.

184

Efficient Component Communication

In Vue.js, communication between components is essential for building interactive applications. There are several methods of component communication, including **props**, **events**, **Vuex**, and **provide/inject**.

Parent-Child Communication

- **Props**: The parent component passes data to a child component via props.
- **Events**: The child component emits events to notify the parent of certain actions.

Example of parent-child communication:

vue

```
<!-- Parent.vue -->
<template>
  <div>
    <child            :message="parentMessage"
@update="updateMessage" />
  </div>
</template>

<script>
import Child from './Child.vue';
```

```
export default {
  components: { Child },
  data() {
    return {
      parentMessage: 'Hello from Parent'
    };
  },
  methods: {
    updateMessage(newMessage) {
      this.parentMessage = newMessage;
    }
  }
};
</script>
vue


<!-- Child.vue -->
<template>
  <div>
    <p>{{ message }}</p>
    <button          @click="sendUpdate">Update
Parent</button>
  </div>
</template>

<script>
export default {
  props: ['message'],
  methods: {
```

```
    sendUpdate() {
      this.$emit('update', 'Updated message from
Child');
    }
  }
};
</script>
```

In this example:

- The parent component passes a `message` prop to the child.
- The child emits an event (`update`) that the parent listens for, updating the parent's data when the button is clicked.

Sibling Communication

To communicate between sibling components, you can use an **Event Bus** or **Vuex** for shared state.

Example using Vuex for sibling communication:

```javascript
// store.js (Vuex)
export const store = new Vuex.Store({
  state: {
    sharedData: 'Hello from Vuex'
  },
```

```
mutations: {
  updateSharedData(state, newData) {
    state.sharedData = newData;
  }
}
});
vue


<!-- ComponentA.vue -->
<template>
  <div>
    <button @click="updateData">Update   Shared
Data</button>
  </div>
</template>

<script>
export default {
  methods: {
    updateData() {
      this.$store.commit('updateSharedData',
'New data from ComponentA');
    }
  }
};
</script>
vue


<!-- ComponentB.vue -->
```

```
<template>
  <div>
    <p>{{ sharedData }}</p>
  </div>
</template>

<script>
export default {
  computed: {
    sharedData() {
      return this.$store.state.sharedData;
    }
  }
};
</script>
```

In this example:

- **ComponentA** updates the shared data using Vuex mutations.
- **ComponentB** reflects the updated data, ensuring synchronized state across components.

Performance Optimization Tips

Vue.js is designed to be fast, but there are several techniques you can use to optimize performance, especially in larger applications with complex state and many components.

Lazy Loading Components

Use Vue's **dynamic `import()`** to lazy-load components only when they are needed. This reduces the initial loading time of your app.

```javascript
const AsyncComponent = () =>
import('@/components/AsyncComponent.vue');

export default {
  components: {
    AsyncComponent
  }
};
```

Avoid Unnecessary Re-renders

Vue.js re-renders components whenever their state or props change. However, unnecessary re-renders can negatively impact performance. To avoid this:

- Use **v-show** instead of **v-if** when elements toggle frequently but don't need to be removed from the DOM.
- Use **key** in v-for loops to help Vue optimize re-renders.

```html
<ul>
```

```
<li  v-for="item  in  items"  :key="item.id">{{
item.name }}</li>
</ul>
```

Debouncing and Throttling

For input fields, search bars, and other user interactions, use **debouncing** or **throttling** techniques to limit the number of times a function is called, improving performance by reducing unnecessary operations.

Example using lodash's debounce:

```javascript
import { debounce } from 'lodash';

export default {
  data() {
    return {
      searchQuery: ''
    };
  },
  methods: {
    search: debounce(function() {
      console.log('Search:', this.searchQuery);
    }, 500)
  }
};
```

Use Vue's `keep-alive` for Caching

When you have components that don't need to be re-rendered every time, use **<keep-alive>** to cache components, improving performance by avoiding unnecessary re-renders.

html

```
<keep-alive>
  <component :is="currentComponent" />
</keep-alive>
```

Summary:

In this chapter, we covered several best practices for **Vue.js development**:

- **Organizing your project structure** to keep your application maintainable and scalable.
- **Code reusability** and **modularization** using small, focused components and Vuex for shared state.
- Efficient **component communication** using props, events, and Vuex for state management.
- Performance optimization tips such as **lazy loading**, **avoiding unnecessary re-renders**, and **debouncing**.

By following these best practices, you can build Vue.js applications that are clean, maintainable, and performant, whether you're working on small projects or large-scale applications.

CHAPTER 16

BUILDING A REAL-WORLD VUE.JS APPLICATION: PART 1

Introduction

In this chapter, we will begin building a **real-world Vue.js application**. We will go step by step through the setup, planning, and implementation of the application. This first part will focus on **project setup**, **creating the initial Vue components**, and **integrating basic functionality** to lay the foundation for a fully functional app.

By the end of this chapter, you will have a basic structure and some core functionality for your application. In the next chapters, we will build upon this structure by adding more features, improving performance, and optimizing for production.

Project Setup and Planning

Before we begin writing any code, it's important to first plan and set up the project. Proper planning ensures that the application remains organized and maintainable as it grows.

Choosing the Project

For this example, let's build a **task management application** where users can:

- View a list of tasks.
- Add new tasks.
- Edit and delete tasks.
- Mark tasks as complete.

This app will be a simple single-page application (SPA) with basic CRUD (Create, Read, Update, Delete) functionality.

Setting Up the Project

To set up a Vue project, you can use **Vue CLI** to create a new project. Vue CLI is a command-line tool that helps you quickly scaffold a Vue.js project with a predefined structure.

1. **Install Vue CLI** (if you haven't installed it already):

bash

```
npm install -g @vue/cli
```

2. **Create a new Vue project**:

bash

```
vue create task-manager
```

You will be prompted to select a preset (for this case, the default preset is fine). Once the project is created, navigate into the project folder:

```bash
cd task-manager
```

3. **Run the development server**:

```bash
npm run serve
```

This will start a local development server at http://localhost:8080, and you can start developing your app there.

Project Directory Structure

By default, Vue CLI creates a project structure like this:

```php
task-manager/
  public/
    index.html        # Main HTML file
  src/
```

195

```
    assets/              # Images and other static
assets
    components/          # Vue components
    App.vue              # Root component
    main.js                 # Entry point for the
application
```

We will primarily work in the `src/components` directory, where we will store our Vue components.

Creating the First Vue Components

Vue applications are made up of **components**. Components are reusable building blocks that control parts of the user interface (UI). We'll start by creating a few components for our task management app.

Creating a Header Component

We'll begin by creating a simple **Header** component for our app.

1. In the `src/components` directory, create a new file named `Header.vue`:

vue

```
<template>
  <header>
    <h1>Task Manager</h1>
```

196

```
  </header>
</template>

<script>
export default {
  name: "Header"
};
</script>

<style scoped>
header {
  background-color: #42b983;
  color: white;
  padding: 20px;
  text-align: center;
}
</style>
```

In this example:

- The `Header` component displays a simple title for our application.
- We apply some basic styling to the header, such as a background color and padding.

Creating a Task List Component

Next, we will create a component to display the list of tasks.

1. In the `src/components` directory, create a new file named `TaskList.vue`:

vue

```
<template>
  <div>
    <h2>Task List</h2>
    <ul>
      <li v-for="task in tasks" :key="task.id">
        {{ task.name }}
        <button
@click="deleteTask(task.id)">Delete</button>
      </li>
    </ul>
  </div>
</template>

<script>
export default {
  name: "TaskList",
  props: {
    tasks: Array
  },
  methods: {
    deleteTask(taskId) {
      this.$emit("delete-task", taskId);
    }
  }
```

```
};
</script>

<style scoped>
ul {
  list-style-type: none;
  padding: 0;
}
li {
  padding: 10px;
  margin: 5px 0;
  background-color: #f0f0f0;
  border-radius: 5px;
}
button {
  background-color: #ff5733;
  color: white;
  border: none;
  padding: 5px 10px;
  cursor: pointer;
  margin-left: 10px;
}
button:hover {
  background-color: #c70039;
}
</style>
```

In this example:

- The `TaskList` component receives an array of tasks through the `tasks` prop.
- It renders each task in a list (`<ul>` and `<li>` elements).
- The component also has a "Delete" button next to each task, which emits an event (`delete-task`) when clicked to notify the parent component that a task needs to be deleted.

Integrating Basic Functionality

Now that we have created the basic components (`Header` and `TaskList`), we can integrate them into the main app and start implementing basic functionality like adding and removing tasks.

Modifying App.vue

The `App.vue` component is the root of the application. We'll modify it to include the `Header` and `TaskList` components, as well as handle adding and removing tasks.

1. In the `src/App.vue` file, update the content as follows:

vue

```
<template>
  <div id="app">
    <Header />
```

```
    <input v-model="newTask" placeholder="Enter
a task" />
    <button @click="addTask">Add Task</button>
    <TaskList     :tasks="tasks"     @delete-
task="removeTask" />
  </div>
</template>

<script>
import Header from './components/Header.vue';
import            TaskList            from
'./components/TaskList.vue';

export default {
  name: 'App',
  components: {
    Header,
    TaskList
  },
  data() {
    return {
      newTask: '',
      tasks: []
    };
  },
  methods: {
    addTask() {
      if (this.newTask.trim()) {
        const task = {
```

```
        id: Date.now(),
         name: this.newTask
       };
       this.tasks.push(task);
       this.newTask = ''; // Clear the input
field after adding the task
     }
   },
   removeTask(taskId) {
     this.tasks = this.tasks.filter(task =>
task.id !== taskId);
   }
  }
};
</script>

<style>
#app {
  font-family: Arial, sans-serif;
  text-align: center;
  padding: 20px;
}
input {
  padding: 10px;
  margin: 10px;
  font-size: 16px;
}
button {
  padding: 10px 20px;
```

```
  font-size: 16px;
  background-color: #42b983;
  color: white;
  border: none;
  cursor: pointer;
}
button:hover {
  background-color: #357a56;
}
</style>
```

Explanation:

- The `App.vue` component includes both the `Header` and `TaskList` components.
- We use `v-model` to bind the `newTask` input field to the component's data.
- The `addTask` method adds a new task to the `tasks` array, and `removeTask` removes a task from the list based on its `id`.
- We pass the `tasks` array to the `TaskList` component as a prop and listen for the `delete-task` event to remove tasks.

Testing the Application

Now, run the development server:

203

```bash
bash

npm run serve
```

Visit `http://localhost:8080` in your browser, and you should see:

- A header with the text "Task Manager".
- An input field to add a new task.
- A list of tasks that can be added and removed.

When you add a task, it should appear in the task list, and when you click "Delete", the task should be removed from the list.

Summary:

In this first part of building a real-world Vue.js application, we:

- Set up the project using Vue CLI.
- Created the `Header` and `TaskList` components.
- Implemented the basic functionality for adding and removing tasks.

In the next part of this series, we will continue building the app by adding more advanced features, such as task editing, persisting data to local storage or an API, and optimizing the app for performance.

This foundation ensures that the app is modular, easy to maintain, and scalable as it grows.

CHAPTER 17

BUILDING A REAL-WORLD VUE.JS APPLICATION: PART 2

Introduction

In this chapter, we will continue building our **task management application** by adding more advanced features. We will focus on:

1. **State management with Vuex** to centralize the application's state and handle data across components.
2. **Fetching data with Vue and Axios** to retrieve tasks from an external API and update the state.
3. **Working with forms and user input** to allow users to create, edit, and delete tasks.

By the end of this chapter, our app will be more interactive, with data persistence and centralized state management, making it more robust and scalable.

State Management with Vuex

State management is essential in larger applications where multiple components need to access or modify the same data. **Vuex** is Vue.js's state management pattern and library that helps manage the state in a centralized store.

Setting Up Vuex

If you haven't already, you need to install **Vuex** in your project:

```bash
npm install vuex
```

Next, we'll create a **Vuex store** to manage the state of the application, including the tasks.

Creating the Vuex Store

1. **Create the store**: In the src/store directory, create a new file index.js:

```javascript
import Vue from 'vue';
import Vuex from 'vuex';

Vue.use(Vuex);

export default new Vuex.Store({
  state: {
    tasks: [],
  },
  mutations: {
    setTasks(state, tasks) {
      state.tasks = tasks;
```

```
    },
    addTask(state, task) {
      state.tasks.push(task);
    },
    removeTask(state, taskId) {
      state.tasks = state.tasks.filter(task =>
task.id !== taskId);
    },
    updateTask(state, updatedTask) {
      const index = state.tasks.findIndex(task
=> task.id === updatedTask.id);
      if (index !== -1) {
        Vue.set(state.tasks,             index,
updatedTask);
      }
    }
  },
  actions: {
    fetchTasks({ commit }) {
      // Here, you can fetch data from an API or
use mock data

axios.get('https://jsonplaceholder.typicode.com
/todos')
        .then(response => {
          commit('setTasks', response.data);
        })
        .catch(error => {
```

```
          console.error('Error fetching tasks:',
error);
        });
    },
    addTask({ commit }, task) {
      commit('addTask', task);
    },
    removeTask({ commit }, taskId) {
      commit('removeTask', taskId);
    },
    updateTask({ commit }, updatedTask) {
      commit('updateTask', updatedTask);
    }
  },
  getters: {
    allTasks(state) {
      return state.tasks;
    }
  }
});
```

Explanation:

- The state object holds the application's data, in this case, the tasks array.

- The mutations are responsible for modifying the state. For instance, setTasks sets the list of tasks, and addTask adds a new task.

- The `actions` are used for asynchronous operations. The `fetchTasks` action fetches tasks from an API and commits the `setTasks` mutation.
- The `getters` allow you to retrieve data from the state. In this case, `allTasks` returns the list of tasks.

Integrating Vuex in `App.vue`

Now, let's modify the `App.vue` file to use the Vuex store for state management. We will connect the store to our components and actions.

1. **Update `App.vue`:**

vue

```
<template>
  <div id="app">
    <Header />
    <input v-model="newTask" placeholder="Enter
a task" />
    <button @click="addTask">Add Task</button>
    <TaskList      :tasks="tasks"      @delete-
task="removeTask" @edit-task="editTask" />
  </div>
</template>

<script>
import Header from './components/Header.vue';
```

```
import                TaskList                from
'./components/TaskList.vue';
import { mapState, mapActions } from 'vuex';

export default {
  name: 'App',
  components: {
    Header,
    TaskList
  },
  data() {
    return {
      newTask: ''
    };
  },
  computed: {
    ...mapState(['tasks'])
  },
  methods: {
    ...mapActions(['addTask',        'removeTask',
'updateTask']),
    addTask() {
      if (this.newTask.trim()) {
        const task = {
          id: Date.now(),
          name: this.newTask,
          completed: false
        };
        this.addTask(task);
```

```
        this.newTask = ''; // Clear the input
field after adding the task
      }
    },
    removeTask(taskId) {
      this.removeTask(taskId);
    },
    editTask(updatedTask) {
      this.updateTask(updatedTask);
    }
  },
  created() {
    this.$store.dispatch('fetchTasks'); // Fetch
tasks when the component is created
  }
};
</script>

<style>
#app {
  font-family: Arial, sans-serif;
  text-align: center;
  padding: 20px;
}
input {
  padding: 10px;
  margin: 10px;
  font-size: 16px;
}
```

```css
button {
  padding: 10px 20px;
  font-size: 16px;
  background-color: #42b983;
  color: white;
  border: none;
  cursor: pointer;
}
button:hover {
  background-color: #357a56;
}
</style>
```

Explanation:

- The `App.vue` now uses **Vuex** for managing the tasks. We connect the `tasks` array from the store using `mapState`.
- The `addTask`, `removeTask`, and `updateTask` methods are mapped to Vuex actions using `mapActions`. These actions will trigger mutations in the Vuex store to modify the task list.
- The `created()` lifecycle hook dispatches the `fetchTasks` action to load tasks from an external API when the app is created.

Fetching Data with Vue and Axios

Fetching data is a common task in web applications, and **Axios** is one of the most popular HTTP clients for handling API requests.

In the previous section, we already set up the `fetchTasks` action in Vuex, which fetches data from an external API (`https://jsonplaceholder.typicode.com/todos`). You can replace the URL with a real API endpoint or use mock data during development.

Using Axios to Fetch Data

In the `fetchTasks` action, we are making an HTTP request using Axios's `get` method:

javascript

```javascript
axios.get('https://jsonplaceholder.typicode.com
/todos')
  .then(response => {
    commit('setTasks', response.data);
  })
  .catch(error => {
    console.error('Error    fetching    tasks:',
error);
  });
```

Once the data is fetched, we commit the `setTasks` mutation to update the store with the retrieved tasks.

Working with Forms and User Input

Handling forms and user input is a core aspect of most web applications. In Vue, you can easily manage form elements using **v-model** for two-way data binding.

In our app, we're using **v-model** to bind the input field for creating new tasks:

vue

```
<input v-model="newTask" placeholder="Enter a task" />
```

This ensures that the `newTask` data property is always in sync with the input field, making it easy to add new tasks.

Additionally, we have a button that calls the `addTask` method when clicked, which creates a new task and adds it to the task list. The method checks that the input is not empty before adding the task to the Vuex store.

Task Editing

To allow task editing, we'll add functionality to modify the task name. This can be done by passing the task object to a child component (e.g., `TaskList`) and allowing the user to edit the task inline.

In the next part of the application, we will implement the functionality to edit tasks in the list and persist the changes.

Summary

In this part of the task management app, we:

- **Set up Vuex** to manage the app's state, including fetching, adding, removing, and updating tasks.
- Used **Axios** to fetch task data from an API and updated the Vuex store.
- Implemented basic **form handling** with `v-model` to capture user input for new tasks.

In the next chapter, we will continue building the app by adding features for editing tasks and persisting data to a back-end server or local storage. We will also look into performance optimization techniques and other enhancements.

CHAPTER 18

BUILDING A REAL-WORLD VUE.JS APPLICATION: PART 3

Introduction

In this part of the series, we will continue to enhance our **task management application** by adding more complex features:

1. **Routing with Vue Router** to manage multiple pages.

2. **Managing user authentication** to allow users to log in and view their personalized tasks.

3. **Structuring the application for scaling**, ensuring that as the app grows, it remains maintainable and efficient.

By the end of this chapter, our app will have multiple views, support user authentication, and be structured to handle growth.

Adding Routing with Vue Router

Vue Router is the official routing library for Vue.js, allowing you to manage navigation between different views or pages in a Vue application. In this section, we will add routing to our app, allowing users to navigate between pages, such as a login page and a task list page.

Installing Vue Router

To start using Vue Router in your project, you first need to install it:

bash

```
npm install vue-router
```

Setting Up Vue Router

1. **Configure Routes**: In the `src/router` directory (create it if it doesn't exist), create a new file called `index.js`:

javascript

```
import Vue from 'vue';
import Router from 'vue-router';
import Home from '@/views/Home.vue';
import Login from '@/views/Login.vue';

Vue.use(Router);

export default new Router({
  routes: [
    {
      path: '/',
      name: 'home',
      component: Home
    },
```

```
  {
    path: '/login',
    name: 'login',
    component: Login
  }
  ]
});
```

Here, we define two routes:

- /: The home page that shows the task list.
- /login: The login page for users to authenticate.

2. **Update the main Vue instance** to use Vue Router:

In src/main.js (or src/main.ts for TypeScript), import and use the Vue Router configuration:

javascript

```
import Vue from 'vue';
import App from './App.vue';
import router from './router';


Vue.config.productionTip = false;


new Vue({
  render: h => h(App),
  router
}).$mount('#app');
```

Creating Views for Routing

Now, let's create the views for the routes we defined.

1. **Home.vue** (for the task list page): Create a new file in the src/views directory called Home.vue:

vue

```
<template>
  <div>
    <h1>Task Manager</h1>
    <button @click="goToLogin">Login</button>
    <TaskList :tasks="tasks" />
  </div>
</template>

<script>
import                TaskList                from
'@/components/TaskList.vue';

export default {
  name: 'Home',
  components: {
    TaskList
  },
  data() {
    return {
```

```
      tasks: [] // Example static tasks or Vuex-
connected tasks
    };
  },
  methods: {
    goToLogin() {
      this.$router.push({ name: 'login' });
    }
  }
};
</script>
```

2. **Login.vue** (for the login page): Create a new file in src/views called Login.vue:

vue

```
<template>
  <div>
    <h1>Login</h1>
    <form @submit.prevent="handleLogin">
      <input                 v-model="username"
placeholder="Username" required />
      <input v-model="password" type="password"
placeholder="Password" required />
      <button type="submit">Login</button>
    </form>
  </div>
</template>
```

```
<script>
export default {
  name: 'Login',
  data() {
    return {
      username: '',
      password: ''
    };
  },
  methods: {
    handleLogin() {
      // Here you would send a request to an API
to authenticate the user
      if    (this.username    ===    'admin'    &&
this.password === 'password') {
        this.$router.push({ name: 'home' });
      } else {
        alert('Invalid credentials');
      }
    }
  }
};
</script>
```

In this setup:

- **Home.vue** displays the task list and has a button to navigate to the login page.

- **Login.vue** allows users to log in by entering a username and password. If successful, it redirects them to the home page.

Using <router-link> for Navigation

Instead of using programmatic navigation (i.e., this.$router.push()), you can use <router-link> for declarative navigation. For example, replace the button in Home.vue with a router-link:

html

```
<router-link to="/login">
  <button>Go to Login</button>
</router-link>
```

Managing User Authentication

In real-world apps, user authentication is critical. For simplicity, we will simulate a basic authentication flow without integrating a backend API. In a more complex app, you would replace this with a real API request for login and store authentication tokens.

Using Vuex for Authentication

Let's manage the authentication state using Vuex. This will allow us to track if a user is logged in and redirect appropriately.

1. Add Authentication State to Vuex Store

In src/store/index.js, add a new module for authentication:

```javascript
export default new Vuex.Store({
  state: {
    isAuthenticated: false,
    user: null
  },
  mutations: {
    login(state, user) {
      state.isAuthenticated = true;
      state.user = user;
    },
    logout(state) {
      state.isAuthenticated = false;
      state.user = null;
    }
  },
  actions: {
    login({ commit }, user) {
      commit('login', user);
    },
    logout({ commit }) {
      commit('logout');
    }
  },
  getters: {
```

```
    isAuthenticated(state) {
      return state.isAuthenticated;
    },
    currentUser(state) {
      return state.user;
    }
  }
});
```

Here, we've added:

- **State**: Tracks whether the user is authenticated and stores user details.
- **Mutations**: Handles login and logout actions.
- **Actions**: Commit the mutations to change the authentication state.
- **Getters**: Provides access to authentication state and current user data.

2. **Update Login.vue to Use Vuex**

Update the Login.vue component to commit the login mutation when the user logs in:

javascript

```
methods: {
  handleLogin() {
```

```
if    (this.username    ===    'admin'    &&
this.password === 'password') {
    this.$store.dispatch('login', { username:
this.username });
    this.$router.push({ name: 'home' });
  } else {
    alert('Invalid credentials');
  }
 }
}
```

3. Restrict Access to Protected Routes

In Home.vue, we can check if the user is authenticated before displaying the task list. If not, we will redirect them to the login page.

javascript

```
created() {
  if (!this.$store.getters.isAuthenticated) {
    this.$router.push({ name: 'login' });
  }
}
```

Structuring Your Application for Scaling

As your app grows, it's important to structure your code so it's maintainable, scalable, and easy to understand. Here are a few tips for structuring your Vue.js application:

1. Organize by Features

Rather than organizing by file types (components, views, etc.), consider organizing by **feature** or **domain**. For example, you could have directories like auth, tasks, and user-profile that contain all relevant components, views, and services related to each feature.

```bash
src/
  auth/
    components/
      LoginForm.vue
      RegisterForm.vue
    views/
      Login.vue
    store/
      auth.js
  tasks/
    components/
      TaskList.vue
      TaskItem.vue
    views/
      TaskDashboard.vue
    store/
      tasks.js
```

2. Separate API Calls and Services

To keep your components clean and reusable, place your API calls in separate **services**. This way, you can call API functions from any component without cluttering them with network logic.

Example API service:

```javascript

// services/taskService.js
import axios from 'axios';

export default {
  getTasks() {
    return
axios.get('https://api.example.com/tasks');
  },
  createTask(task) {
    return
axios.post('https://api.example.com/tasks',
task);
  }
};
```

3. Use Vuex Modules for Large Applications

If your application has many features (e.g., authentication, tasks, user settings), consider using **Vuex modules**. This allows you to group related state, mutations, actions, and getters into separate modules, keeping your store organized.

javascript

```
// store/modules/tasks.js
export default {
  state: { tasks: [] },
  mutations: {   setTasks(state,   tasks)  {
state.tasks = tasks; } },
  actions: { fetchTasks({ commit }) { /* fetch
tasks logic */ } },
  getters:   {   allTasks(state)   {   return
state.tasks; } }
};
```

Summary

In this chapter, we:

- **Added routing** with Vue Router to manage different pages in the application.
- Implemented **user authentication** with Vuex, simulating login functionality and protecting routes.
- Structured the application for scaling, using Vuex modules, API services, and organizing by features.

In the next chapter, we will enhance the application with features such as task editing, persistence with a backend API, and improve performance by lazy-loading components and optimizing the app.

229

CHAPTER 19

VUE.JS AND RESPONSIVE WEB DESIGN

Introduction to Responsive Web Design

Responsive Web Design (RWD) is a design approach aimed at making web pages look good on a variety of devices, from desktop monitors to mobile phones. The core principle of responsive design is that the layout should adapt to the screen size, orientation, and resolution, ensuring a seamless user experience across all platforms.

With responsive web design, you can:

1. Create a flexible grid layout that adjusts based on the screen size.
2. Use CSS media queries to apply styles based on device characteristics (e.g., screen width, resolution).
3. Ensure that images and other media scale appropriately.
4. Make sure the user interface (UI) is optimized for mobile devices with touch interactions.

In Vue.js, integrating responsive design is straightforward. Since Vue is primarily concerned with the user interface and behavior of the app, making it responsive mainly involves managing layout using CSS and Vue's reactive features, like computed properties, to adjust the display based on the viewport.

Making Your Vue App Mobile-Friendly

Making a Vue.js app mobile-friendly involves using a combination of flexible layouts, CSS media queries, and Vue's component structure. Below are some steps you can take to make your Vue app mobile-friendly:

1. Use a Fluid Grid Layout

A fluid grid layout is based on percentages rather than fixed pixel values. This allows the layout to adjust proportionally based on the screen width. CSS Grid and Flexbox are excellent tools for creating fluid, flexible layouts in Vue.js.

Example of a fluid grid layout using CSS Flexbox:

vue

```
<template>
  <div class="container">
    <div class="item">Item 1</div>
    <div class="item">Item 2</div>
    <div class="item">Item 3</div>
  </div>
</template>
```

```
<style scoped>
.container {
  display: flex;
  justify-content: space-around;
  flex-wrap: wrap;
}

.item {
  flex: 1 1 30%; /* Each item takes 30% of the
width, wrapping when needed */
  margin: 10px;
  background-color: lightgray;
  padding: 20px;
  text-align: center;
}
</style>
```

In this example:

- The .container uses display: flex to arrange the child .item elements in a row. The flex-wrap: wrap allows the items to wrap when the screen size reduces.
- The .item elements take up 30% of the container width, and the layout adapts automatically when the screen size changes.

2. Use Scalable Fonts and Flexible Media

When designing for different screen sizes, you want to ensure that the text, images, and other media elements scale appropriately. Avoid using fixed pixel sizes for fonts and instead use relative units like em, rem, and percentages for better scalability.

For images, ensure that they are responsive by using CSS to limit the width to 100% of their container.

Example of responsive text and images:

vue

```
<template>
  <div class="content">
    <h1 class="title">Welcome to My Blog</h1>
    <img src="blog-image.jpg" alt="Blog Image" class="responsive-image" />
  </div>
</template>

<style scoped>
.title {
  font-size: 2rem; /* Scalable font size */
}

.responsive-image {
```

```
  width: 100%; /* Make the image scale with its
container */
  height: auto; /* Maintain aspect ratio */
}
</style>
```

3. Use Viewport Units for Responsive Typography

Viewport units (vw, vh) are based on the size of the viewport. For example, 1vw is equal to 1% of the viewport's width. Using viewport units allows typography to adjust dynamically based on screen size.

Example of responsive typography:

vue

```
<template>
  <div>
    <h1    class="responsive-heading">Responsive
Heading</h1>
  </div>
</template>

<style scoped>
.responsive-heading {
  font-size: 8vw; /* Font size based on viewport
width */
}
</style>
```

This will make the font size responsive, growing or shrinking depending on the width of the browser window.

Working with Media Queries in Vue.js

Media queries are the cornerstone of responsive web design. They allow you to apply different CSS rules depending on the characteristics of the device, such as screen width, height, or orientation. Vue.js doesn't directly deal with media queries, but you can use them in your component styles or with computed properties to change the layout or behavior of the app based on the screen size.

1. Using Media Queries in Component Styles

You can use CSS media queries directly in your Vue component styles to apply specific styles for different screen sizes.

Example of media queries in Vue component:

vue

```vue
<template>
  <div class="container">
    <h1 class="title">Responsive Title</h1>
  </div>
</template>

<style scoped>
```

```css
.title {
  font-size: 24px;
}


@media (max-width: 600px) {
  .title {
    font-size: 18px; /* Smaller font size for
mobile screens */
  }
}
</style>
```

In this example:

- The `.title` class has a default font size of `24px`.
- When the screen width is less than `600px` (i.e., for mobile devices), the font size will change to `18px`.

2. Using Vue's Computed Properties with Media Queries

While media queries in CSS are useful, sometimes you might want to dynamically adjust certain behaviors in Vue components based on screen size. In that case, you can use Vue's **computed properties** along with JavaScript to detect the viewport size and adjust your components' behavior.

Example of using computed properties to check the screen width:

vue

```
<template>
  <div>
    <p v-if="isMobile">This is a mobile view</p>
    <p v-else>This is a desktop view</p>
  </div>
</template>

<script>
export default {
  computed: {
    isMobile() {
      return window.innerWidth <= 600; // Check
if the screen width is 600px or less
    }
  },
  mounted() {
    window.addEventListener('resize',
this.handleResize);
  },
  methods: {
    handleResize() {
      this.$forceUpdate(); // Trigger reactivity
on window resize
    }
  }
};
</script>
```

In this example:

237

- We use a computed property `isMobile` to check if the window width is less than or equal to `600px`.
- The component automatically updates when the window is resized due to the `resize` event listener.
- Depending on the screen size, we display either a mobile or desktop view.

Real-World Example: Making a Blog Responsive

In this real-world example, we will make a simple **blog page** responsive. The blog will include:

- A header with the blog title and navigation links.
- A list of blog posts.
- A sidebar with additional information.

1. Template for the Blog Page

vue

```vue
<template>
  <div>
    <header class="header">
      <h1>My Blog</h1>
      <nav>
        <router-link    to="/home">Home</router-link>
        <router-link  to="/about">About</router-link>
```

```
      </nav>
    </header>

    <div class="content">
      <aside class="sidebar">
        <h2>Sidebar</h2>
        <p>Additional blog info here.</p>
      </aside>

      <main class="main-content">
        <h2>Blog Posts</h2>
        <div class="post">
          <h3>Post Title 1</h3>
          <p>Content of the blog post goes
here...</p>
        </div>
        <div class="post">
          <h3>Post Title 2</h3>
          <p>Content of the blog post goes
here...</p>
        </div>
      </main>
    </div>
  </div>
</template>

<style scoped>
.header {
  background-color: #42b983;
```

```css
  padding: 20px;
  color: white;
  text-align: center;
}

nav a {
  margin: 10px;
  color: white;
  text-decoration: none;
}

.content {
  display: flex;
  justify-content: space-between;
  margin: 20px;
}

.sidebar {
  width: 25%;
  background-color: #f4f4f4;
  padding: 20px;
}

.main-content {
  width: 70%;
}

.post {
  background-color: #fff;
```

```css
  padding: 10px;
  margin-bottom: 20px;
}

@media (max-width: 768px) {
  .content {
    flex-direction: column;
    align-items: center;
  }

  .sidebar {
    width: 100%;
    margin-bottom: 20px;
  }

  .main-content {
    width: 100%;
  }
}

@media (max-width: 480px) {
  .header h1 {
    font-size: 1.5rem;
  }

  .post h3 {
    font-size: 1.2rem;
  }
}
```

```
</style>
```

Explanation:

- The header contains a blog title and navigation links to different pages.
- The content is divided into a sidebar and a main content area using Flexbox. On smaller screens (`max-width: 768px`), the layout switches to a column, and the sidebar becomes full-width.
- On very small screens (`max-width: 480px`), the font sizes are reduced to make the content more readable on mobile devices.

2. Making the Blog Responsive

The CSS includes two key media queries:

- **`max-width: 768px`**: This applies styles for tablets and smaller screens, stacking the sidebar and main content vertically.
- **`max-width: 480px`**: This applies styles for mobile devices, reducing the font size for better readability on small screens.

With this responsive layout, the blog will adjust seamlessly to different screen sizes, ensuring that it's mobile-friendly.

Summary

In this chapter, we explored **responsive web design** in the context of Vue.js:

- We learned how to make a Vue app **mobile-friendly** by using flexible grid layouts and responsive typography.
- We worked with **media queries** to apply different styles based on the device's screen size.
- We created a **real-world example** by building a responsive blog page with a header, sidebar, and main content that adapts to mobile and desktop views.

By implementing responsive design principles in your Vue.js app, you can create user-friendly interfaces that work well across devices, ensuring a consistent and optimal experience for all users.

CHAPTER 20

HANDLING USER AUTHENTICATION IN VUE.JS

Introduction to Authentication

Authentication is a process by which an application verifies the identity of a user. It's a critical aspect of any web application that handles sensitive data or performs personalized actions for users, such as a blog, e-commerce platform, or task management app.

There are many ways to implement authentication, but one of the most popular methods for securing modern web applications is using **JSON Web Tokens (JWT)**. JWT provides a stateless mechanism for securely transmitting information between the client and server.

In this chapter, we will explore:

- The basics of user authentication in Vue.js.
- How to use **JWT (JSON Web Tokens)** for secure user authentication.
- How to **protect routes** and manage **user sessions** in Vue.js.
- A real-world example of implementing a **login and registration system** using JWT.

Using JWT (JSON Web Tokens) for User Authentication

JWT (JSON Web Tokens) is an open standard (RFC 7519) that defines a compact and self-contained way to securely transmit information between parties as a JSON object. JWTs are commonly used in authentication systems where users log in, and the server generates a token for the client to use in subsequent requests.

How JWT Works

1. **User Login**: The user submits their login credentials (e.g., username and password) to the server.
2. **Token Generation**: The server verifies the credentials and, if valid, generates a JWT containing a payload (e.g., user ID and role). The token is signed with a secret key.
3. **Token Storage**: The client (browser) stores the token, usually in localStorage or sessionStorage.
4. **Authenticated Requests**: For subsequent requests, the client sends the JWT in the `Authorization` header as a bearer token.
5. **Token Verification**: The server verifies the token's validity and allows access to protected resources.

JWTs are typically used in a stateless, sessionless authentication system. Once the token is issued, the server does not need to

245

maintain any session state between requests, making it scalable and easy to implement.

JWT Structure

A JWT consists of three parts:

1. **Header**: Contains metadata about the token (e.g., type and signing algorithm).
2. **Payload**: Contains the claims or user-specific data.
3. **Signature**: Ensures the token's integrity and authenticity.

Example of a JWT:

```
eyJhbGciOiJIUzI1NiIsInR5cCI6IkpXVCJ9.eyJzdWIiOi
IxMjM0NTY3ODkwIiwibmFtZSI6IkpvaG4gRG9lIiwiaWF0I
joxNTE2MjM5MDIyfQ.SflKxwRJSMeKKF2QT4fwpMeJf36PO
k6yJV_adQssw5c
```

Protecting Routes and Managing User Sessions

In a Vue.js application, **protected routes** refer to routes that require the user to be authenticated before they can access them. For example, an authenticated user should be able to view the task list, but a guest should not.

Using Vue Router for Route Protection

To protect routes, we can use **Vue Router** along with **navigation guards**. A navigation guard allows us to check if the user is authenticated before allowing them to access a certain route.

1. **Create a Route Guard for Protected Routes** In your router configuration (`src/router/index.js`), add a route guard to check if the user is authenticated before accessing protected routes:

javascript

```javascript
import Vue from 'vue';
import Router from 'vue-router';
import Home from '@/views/Home.vue';
import Login from '@/views/Login.vue';
import store from '@/store'; // Vuex store for
managing authentication state

Vue.use(Router);

const routes = [
  {
    path: '/',
    name: 'home',
    component: Home,
    meta: { requiresAuth: true } // This route
requires authentication
```

```
  },
  {
    path: '/login',
    name: 'login',
    component: Login
  }
];

const router = new Router({
  routes
});

// Route guard to check authentication
router.beforeEach((to, from, next) => {
  if        (to.matched.some(record        =>
record.meta.requiresAuth)) {
    if (!store.getters.isAuthenticated) {
      // If not authenticated, redirect to login
      next({ name: 'login' });
    } else {
      next();
    }
  } else {
    next(); // Always call next() to allow the
route
  }
});

export default router;
```

In this code:

- We add a `meta` field to the routes we want to protect, in this case, the `home` route.
- The `beforeEach` navigation guard checks if the route requires authentication and whether the user is authenticated (we're checking the `isAuthenticated` getter from Vuex).
- If the user is not authenticated, they are redirected to the login page.

Managing User Sessions with Vuex

To manage the user's authentication state globally, we will use Vuex. We'll store the user's authentication status (whether they are logged in or not) in Vuex.

1. **Vuex Store for Authentication** In `src/store/index.js`, we will create a module to manage the authentication state:

javascript

```
import Vue from 'vue';
import Vuex from 'vuex';

Vue.use(Vuex);
```

```
export default new Vuex.Store({
  state: {
    isAuthenticated: false,
    user: null,
    token: null
  },
  mutations: {
    setAuthenticated(state, { user, token }) {
      state.isAuthenticated = true;
      state.user = user;
      state.token = token;
    },
    logout(state) {
      state.isAuthenticated = false;
      state.user = null;
      state.token = null;
    }
  },
  actions: {
    login({ commit }, { user, token }) {
      commit('setAuthenticated', { user, token
});
    },
    logout({ commit }) {
      commit('logout');
    }
  },
  getters: {
```

```
    isAuthenticated:           state           =>
state.isAuthenticated,
    currentUser: state => state.user,
    authToken: state => state.token
  }
});
```

In this Vuex store:

- **State** holds the authentication status (isAuthenticated), the user object (user), and the JWT (token).
- **Mutations** allow updating the state. The setAuthenticated mutation sets the user and token when they log in, and the logout mutation clears the state when they log out.
- **Actions** commit the mutations. The login action sets the authentication state, while logout clears it.
- **Getters** provide access to the state, such as checking if the user is authenticated (isAuthenticated).

Storing the Token

The token should be stored securely in the browser. For simplicity, we'll use localStorage to persist the token between page reloads.

```
javascript
```

```
// In login action or method:
localStorage.setItem('authToken', token); //
Store the token
```

When the app reloads, we can retrieve the token and set the authentication state:

```
javascript
```

```
// On app initialization or Vuex store
initialization:
const token = localStorage.getItem('authToken');
if (token) {
  // If token exists, assume user is
authenticated and set state
  store.commit('setAuthenticated', { user: {
username: 'admin' }, token });
}
```

Real-World Example: Login and Registration System

In this example, we will create a simple **login and registration system** that uses JWT for authentication. The system will allow users to log in, view protected content, and log out.

1. **Login.vue**

```
vue
```

```
<template>
  <div>
    <h1>Login</h1>
    <form @submit.prevent="handleLogin">
      <input                    v-model="username"
placeholder="Username" required />
      <input v-model="password" type="password"
placeholder="Password" required />
      <button type="submit">Login</button>
    </form>
  </div>
</template>

<script>
import { mapActions } from 'vuex';

export default {
  data() {
    return {
      username: '',
      password: ''
    };
  },
  methods: {
    ...mapActions(['login']),
    handleLogin() {
      // Simulate an API call to authenticate the
user
```

```
    const token = 'fake-jwt-token'; // This
should be received from the server
    this.login({    user:    {    username:
this.username }, token });
    this.$router.push({ name: 'home' });
  }
 }
};
</script>
```

2. **Home.vue**

vue

```
<template>
  <div>
    <h1>Welcome, {{ user.username }}</h1>
    <button @click="logout">Logout</button>
    <div v-if="isAuthenticated">
      <p>This is a protected content section.</p>
    </div>
  </div>
</template>

<script>
import { mapState, mapActions } from 'vuex';

export default {
  computed: {
    ...mapState(['user', 'isAuthenticated'])
```

```
  },
  methods: {
    ...mapActions(['logout']),
  }
};
</script>
```

3. **App.vue** Wrap everything in the `App.vue`:

vue

```
<template>
  <div id="app">
    <router-view></router-view>
  </div>
</template>

<script>
export default {
  name: 'App',
};
</script>
```

In this example:

- The `Login.vue` component simulates a login action, storing the JWT and user data in Vuex and redirecting to the home page.

255

- The `Home.vue` component checks if the user is authenticated and displays protected content.
- We use Vuex to manage the authentication state globally, including login, logout, and route protection.

Summary

In this chapter, we:

- Introduced **JWT** for secure user authentication.
- Protected routes using **Vue Router** and **Vuex** to manage user sessions.
- Implemented a simple **login and registration system** using JWT to simulate authentication.

With Vue.js, you can easily manage user authentication using Vuex for state management and Vue Router for protecting routes. In the next chapter, we will explore more advanced authentication patterns and features, such as role-based access control and refreshing JWTs.

CHAPTER 21

DEPLOYING VUE.JS APPLICATIONS

Introduction

Once you've built a Vue.js application, the next step is to get it out to the world by deploying it to a hosting platform. Deployment involves preparing your app for production, choosing a hosting service, and ensuring that your app performs efficiently in a real-world environment.

In this chapter, we will walk through the steps to:

1. **Prepare your Vue app for production**.
2. **Use Vue CLI for deployment**.
3. **Deploy your app to popular hosting services** like Netlify and Heroku.
4. A **real-world example** of deploying a simple **To-Do List app**.

By the end of this chapter, you will be able to deploy a Vue.js application and have it accessible on the web.

Preparing Your Vue App for Production

Before deploying your Vue.js app, you need to ensure that it's optimized for production. This involves building a production-ready version of your app with Vue CLI.

1. Building for Production

Vue CLI provides a simple command to build your app for production. The build process optimizes your app by minifying JavaScript, optimizing assets, and ensuring that your app is ready to be served on a production server.

To prepare your app for production, run the following command:

```bash
npm run build
```

This command will:

- Generate a **dist/ (distribution)** folder that contains the optimized, minified version of your app.
- Minify the JavaScript, CSS, and HTML files.
- Optimize images and other assets.
- Create a `index.html` that links to the minified scripts and styles.

2. Understanding the Build Folder

Once the build process is complete, the output will be in the `dist/` folder (by default). This folder contains all the files that need to be served by the web server. Inside the `dist/` folder, you will find:

- **index.html**: The main HTML file that loads the app.
- **js/**: A folder containing your JavaScript files (e.g., `app.js`, `vendor.js`).
- **css/**: A folder with the minified CSS files.
- **img/**: A folder with optimized images and assets.

This is the folder you will upload to your hosting service for deployment.

Using Vue CLI for Deployment

Vue CLI simplifies the process of deploying your Vue.js application by automating common tasks like building the app for production, managing environment variables, and setting up the deployment configurations.

1. Setting up Environment Variables

Sometimes, you might need to use different configurations for development and production (e.g., API URLs). You can set up environment variables to manage these configurations.

1. **Create a `.env.production` file** to store your production-specific configurations, such as API endpoints or any other variables:

```
env
```

```
VUE_APP_API_URL=https://api.example.com
```

2. **Access environment variables** in your Vue components:

```
javascript
```

```
console.log(process.env.VUE_APP_API_URL);    //
Will output the production API URL
```

2. Customizing the `vue.config.js` File

You can customize the Vue CLI's build and dev server configurations by creating a `vue.config.js` file at the root of your project. For example, you can specify the **publicPath** (where the app will be hosted), or configure a proxy for API requests during development.

Example of a `vue.config.js` file:

```
javascript
```

```
module.exports = {
  publicPath: '/my-vue-app/', // The base URL for
the deployed app
```

```
devServer: {
    proxy: 'https://api.example.com', // Proxy
API requests to the backend during development
  },
};
```

3. Running the Build Command Again

After setting up your configurations, run the build command again to ensure everything is prepared for deployment:

```bash
```

```
npm run build
```

Once the build is complete, your app is ready to be deployed.

Deploying to Popular Hosting Services (e.g., Netlify, Heroku)

Now that we have built our production-ready app, let's deploy it to a hosting service. We'll cover two popular hosting options for Vue.js applications: **Netlify** and **Heroku**.

1. Deploying to Netlify

Netlify is a popular platform for deploying modern web applications. It is especially well-suited for static sites like Vue.js apps, and it offers continuous deployment from GitHub or GitLab.

Steps to Deploy to Netlify

1. **Push your code to GitHub**:
   - If your Vue app isn't already in a Git repository, initialize a new repository on GitHub and push your local project to GitHub.
2. **Create a Netlify account** and log in.
3. **Click "New Site from Git"** on the Netlify dashboard.
4. **Connect your GitHub repository** to Netlify.
5. **Select the branch** you want to deploy (usually `main` or `master`).
6. **Configure build settings**:
   - **Build command**: `npm run build`
   - **Publish directory**: `dist/`
7. **Click "Deploy site"**. Netlify will automatically build and deploy your app.

After the deployment is complete, Netlify will provide you with a unique URL where your Vue app is hosted. You can also configure a custom domain if desired.

2. Deploying to Heroku

Heroku is a platform-as-a-service (PaaS) that allows you to deploy apps without managing the infrastructure. Heroku can deploy Vue apps, although it is more commonly used for full-stack apps.

Steps to Deploy to Heroku

1. **Install Heroku CLI**: Download and install the Heroku CLI from the Heroku website.

2. **Log in to Heroku**:

   bash

   ```
   heroku login
   ```

3. **Initialize a Git repository** (if not already initialized):

   bash

   ```
   git init
   git add .
   git commit -m "Initial commit"
   ```

4. **Create a Heroku app**:

   bash

   ```
   heroku create my-vue-app
   ```

5. **Add a `static` buildpack**: Since Vue.js is a static site, use the `static` buildpack to serve the `dist` folder.

   bash

```
heroku                          buildpacks:set
https://github.com/heroku/heroku-
buildpack-static
```

6. **Add a `static.json` file** to the root of the project to tell Heroku how to serve the app:

```json
json

{
  "root": "dist/",
  "routes": {
    "/**": "index.html"
  }
}
```

7. **Deploy the app**: Push your code to Heroku using Git:

```bash
bash

git push heroku master
```

8. **Open the app**: Once the deployment is complete, open your app by running:

```bash
bash

heroku open
```

Heroku will now serve your Vue app, and you'll be given a URL where the app is accessible.

Real-World Example: Deploying a To-Do List App

Let's take a **To-Do List app** that we built in previous chapters and deploy it to Netlify.

1. **Prepare the app for production** using `npm run build`.
2. **Push the app to GitHub** if it's not already there.
3. **Follow the steps** in the **Netlify** deployment section to link your GitHub repository to Netlify.
4. **Configure build settings** as discussed, setting the build command to `npm run build` and the publish directory to `dist/`.
5. **Deploy and test** your app by visiting the URL provided by Netlify.

This deployment process can also be applied to more complex applications as you continue to grow and scale your app.

Summary

In this chapter, we:

- Learned how to prepare a Vue.js application for production, using Vue CLI's build command.

- Deployed our app to **Netlify** and **Heroku**, two popular hosting platforms, and covered the steps involved in deploying to both.

- Walked through a real-world example of deploying a simple **To-Do List app** to Netlify.

Deploying Vue.js applications is a straightforward process, and tools like Netlify and Heroku make it easy to host and manage your app. In the next chapter, we will explore advanced topics such as integrating back-end services with Vue.js, handling environment-specific configurations, and implementing continuous integration/continuous deployment (CI/CD) pipelines.

CHAPTER 22

VUE.JS PERFORMANCE OPTIMIZATION

Introduction

As your Vue.js application grows in complexity, performance can become a concern. Ensuring that your app runs efficiently on a variety of devices (from desktop computers to mobile phones) is essential for providing a smooth user experience. In this chapter, we'll explore **common performance bottlenecks, lazy loading, code splitting, caching,** and **efficient data fetching** in Vue.js.

By optimizing your Vue.js app, you can ensure faster loading times, smoother interactions, and an overall better user experience.

In this chapter, we will cover:

- **Common performance bottlenecks** in Vue.js.
- **Lazy loading and code splitting** to reduce the size of the initial bundle.
- **Caching** and **efficient data fetching** to optimize network requests.
- A **real-world example** of optimizing a **news feed app**.

267

Common Performance Bottlenecks in Vue.js

While Vue.js is a very performant framework, certain practices or patterns can lead to performance issues. Some common performance bottlenecks include:

1. Large Component Re-renders

Vue.js re-renders components whenever their state or props change. However, re-rendering large components or deeply nested components can cause performance issues, especially when updates occur frequently.

Solution: To prevent unnecessary re-renders, you can:

- Use **computed properties** to cache expensive calculations.
- Use **v-show** instead of **v-if** for toggling visibility of elements that are likely to change frequently.
- Use the **key attribute** in `v-for` loops to help Vue optimize re-renders.

2. Excessive Data Binding

Excessive data binding can lead to performance issues, especially with large datasets. When you bind large arrays or objects to the DOM, Vue needs to track changes, which can result in slower rendering times.

Solution: Use **virtual scrolling** or **lazy loading** for large lists to render only the visible items.

3. Unoptimized Event Listeners

Event listeners on large numbers of elements can cause performance issues. Vue binds events to elements using a reactive system, so handling a large number of events can become inefficient.

Solution: Debounce or throttle events where necessary (e.g., for scrolling or resize events). Additionally, **event delegation** can be useful for managing large numbers of events on similar elements.

4. Inefficient Data Fetching

Fetching large amounts of data or making multiple requests during the initial load can slow down your app. This issue often occurs when the app fetches all data at once, even if not all of it is immediately needed.

Solution: Use **lazy loading**, **pagination**, and **data caching** to fetch data in smaller chunks as needed.

Lazy Loading and Code Splitting

Lazy loading and code splitting are important strategies for improving the performance of modern web applications. They

269

allow you to load parts of the application only when necessary, rather than loading everything upfront.

1. Lazy Loading in Vue.js

Lazy loading refers to loading parts of your application only when they are needed, such as components, views, or routes. Vue CLI supports lazy loading out of the box via dynamic imports.

In Vue Router, you can use **dynamic imports** to lazy-load route components.

Example:

```javascript
const Home = () => import('@/views/Home.vue');
const About = () => import('@/views/About.vue');

const routes = [
  { path: '/', component: Home },
  { path: '/about', component: About }
];
```

In this example, Vue will automatically load the Home and About components only when the user navigates to the corresponding route. This reduces the initial loading time of your app by splitting the code into smaller chunks.

2. Code Splitting

Code splitting allows you to split your JavaScript bundle into smaller files that can be loaded on demand. This is particularly useful for large applications that have many features and dependencies.

Vue CLI automatically supports code splitting with webpack. By using dynamic imports (`import()`), Vue creates separate JavaScript files for each component or route, which are loaded on demand.

Example of code splitting in Vue Router with lazy loading:

javascript

```javascript
const NewsFeed = () => import('@/views/NewsFeed.vue');
const Profile = () => import('@/views/Profile.vue');

const routes = [
  { path: '/news', component: NewsFeed },
  { path: '/profile', component: Profile }
];
```

In this example, the `NewsFeed` and `Profile` components will only be loaded when the user navigates to /news or /profile, respectively. This reduces the initial bundle size and speeds up the app's load time.

Caching and Efficient Data Fetching

Efficient data fetching and caching are essential for reducing the number of network requests and improving performance. In this section, we'll look at how to optimize data fetching and cache responses to minimize redundant requests.

1. Caching API Responses

To avoid redundant API calls and improve performance, you can cache responses in the browser (e.g., using **localStorage**, **sessionStorage**, or **IndexedDB**). This is especially useful for data that doesn't change often.

Example of caching API responses:

javascript

```
// Fetch data with caching in localStorage
async function fetchTasks() {
  const              cachedTasks              =
localStorage.getItem('tasks');

  if (cachedTasks) {
    return   JSON.parse(cachedTasks);   //   Use
cached data if available
```

```
}

const          response          =          await
axios.get('https://api.example.com/tasks');
  const tasks = response.data;

  // Cache the fetched tasks in localStorage
  localStorage.setItem('tasks',
JSON.stringify(tasks));

  return tasks;
}
```

In this example:

- We first check if the tasks are already cached in localStorage. If they are, we return the cached data.
- If not, we fetch the data from the API and cache the response for future use.

2. Debouncing and Throttling Requests

When making multiple API requests based on user input (e.g., search suggestions), it's important to avoid overwhelming the server with too many requests. **Debouncing** and **throttling** help limit the number of requests made within a certain time period.

Example of debouncing search input:

273

```javascript

import { debounce } from 'lodash';

export default {
  data() {
    return {
      searchQuery: ''
    };
  },
  methods: {
    search: debounce(function() {
      console.log('Searching                    for:',
this.searchQuery);
      // Make the API request here
    }, 500) // 500ms debounce delay
  }
};
```

In this example, the search method is debounced to limit the number of API requests made when the user types in the search field. The request is sent only after the user stops typing for 500ms.

3. Pagination and Infinite Scrolling

For applications with large datasets (e.g., news feeds, product lists), loading all data at once can be inefficient. Use **pagination** or **infinite scrolling** to load data in smaller chunks as needed.

Example of pagination:

```javascript
data() {
  return {
    tasks: [],
    currentPage: 1,
    itemsPerPage: 10
  };
},
methods: {
  fetchTasks() {

axios.get(`https://api.example.com/tasks?page=$
{this.currentPage}&limit=${this.itemsPerPage}`)
      .then(response => {
        this.tasks = response.data;
      })
      .catch(error => console.error(error));
  }
}
```

In this example, the `fetchTasks` method fetches a specific page of tasks, reducing the load on the server and making the app more responsive.

Real-World Example: Optimizing a News Feed App

Let's consider a **news feed app** that displays a list of articles. The app should be optimized for performance by:

- Lazy-loading articles.
- Caching articles to avoid redundant API requests.
- Using pagination or infinite scrolling to load more articles as the user scrolls.

1. Lazy Loading Articles

Use dynamic imports to lazy-load the article components when the user scrolls to the bottom.

vue

```
<template>
  <div>
    <ArticleList :articles="articles" />
    <button       @click="loadMore">Load      More
Articles</button>
  </div>
</template>

<script>
import { debounce } from 'lodash';

export default {
```

```
data() {
  return {
    articles: [],
    currentPage: 1
  };
},
methods: {
  loadMore() {
    this.currentPage++;
    this.fetchArticles();
  },
  fetchArticles: debounce(function() {

axios.get(`https://api.example.com/articles?page=${this.currentPage}`)
      .then(response => {
        this.articles.push(...response.data);
      })
      .catch(error => console.error(error));
  }, 500)
},
mounted() {
  this.fetchArticles();
}
};
</script>
```

In this example:

- We use **debouncing** to reduce the number of API calls when fetching articles.
- The `loadMore` method is used to load additional articles when the user clicks the "Load More" button.

2. Caching Articles

Cache the list of articles in `localStorage` to avoid fetching the same articles again when the user returns to the app.

javascript

```javascript
async function fetchArticles() {
  const            cachedArticles              =
localStorage.getItem('articles');

  if (cachedArticles) {
    return JSON.parse(cachedArticles); // Return
cached articles
  }

  const          response          =          await
axios.get('https://api.example.com/articles');
  const articles = response.data;

  // Cache the articles in localStorage
  localStorage.setItem('articles',
JSON.stringify(articles));
```

```
  return articles;
}
```

3. Infinite Scrolling

Use **infinite scrolling** to load articles as the user scrolls down, instead of using a "Load More" button.

```javascript
mounted() {
  window.addEventListener('scroll',
this.handleScroll);
  this.fetchArticles();
},
methods: {
  handleScroll() {
    if (window.innerHeight + window.scrollY >=
document.body.offsetHeight) {
      this.loadMore();
    }
  }
}
```

In this example, when the user reaches the bottom of the page, more articles are loaded automatically.

Summary

In this chapter, we learned how to optimize the performance of Vue.js applications by addressing common performance bottlenecks, including:

- **Lazy loading and code splitting** to reduce the initial bundle size.
- **Caching** and **efficient data fetching** to minimize unnecessary network requests.
- Techniques like **debouncing**, **pagination**, and **infinite scrolling** to optimize large datasets.

In the real-world example, we optimized a **news feed app** by implementing lazy loading, caching, and infinite scrolling to improve performance. These techniques ensure that the app remains fast and responsive even as the dataset grows.

In the next chapter, we will explore more advanced Vue.js topics, such as integrating with backend services, handling real-time data, and optimizing for SEO.

CHAPTER 23

SECURITY IN VUE.JS APPLICATIONS

Introduction

As web applications become increasingly sophisticated, securing them against potential threats is paramount. Front-end frameworks like Vue.js, while focusing on user interface and experience, also play an essential role in the security of web applications. Vue.js applications, like all modern web apps, are vulnerable to various security risks, including **Cross-Site Scripting (XSS)**, **Cross-Site Request Forgery (CSRF)**, and insecure API interactions.

In this chapter, we will cover:

1. **Security best practices** for front-end development in Vue.js.
2. Techniques for preventing **XSS** and **CSRF** attacks.
3. How to make **secure API calls** and handle **authentication securely**.
4. A **real-world example** of securing an **e-commerce app**.

By the end of this chapter, you will understand how to secure your Vue.js applications against common vulnerabilities and ensure safe and efficient data handling.

Security Best Practices for Front-End Development

When developing front-end applications in Vue.js (or any other framework), there are several fundamental security best practices to follow:

1. Avoiding Inline JavaScript

Avoid using inline JavaScript, such as event handlers like `onclick`, `onload`, and other inline script attributes. Inline JavaScript can open doors for attackers to inject malicious scripts (XSS attacks).

Example of **bad practice**:

html

```
<button    onclick="alert('XSS    Attack')">Click
Me</button>
```

Better approach:

vue

```
<template>
```

```
<button @click="showAlert">Click Me</button>
</template>

<script>
export default {
  methods: {
    showAlert() {
      alert('Hello!');
    }
  }
};
</script>
```

Using Vue's event handling system ensures the script stays separate from the HTML, making it safer from XSS risks.

2. Sanitize User Inputs

Never trust user inputs directly. Always sanitize inputs before rendering them on the page, especially when dealing with data that will be used to generate HTML content (e.g., comments, product descriptions).

You can use libraries like **DOMPurify** to sanitize user inputs:

bash

```
npm install dompurify
javascript
```

```
import DOMPurify from 'dompurify';

const            sanitizedInput            =
DOMPurify.sanitize(userInput);
```

3. Secure Cookies

When using cookies for authentication (e.g., storing JWT tokens), always set the following flags:

- **HttpOnly**: Ensures the cookie cannot be accessed by JavaScript.
- **Secure**: Ensures the cookie is sent only over HTTPS.
- **SameSite**: Prevents the cookie from being sent with cross-origin requests.

Example of setting a secure cookie:

```
javascript

document.cookie = "token=your-jwt-token; Secure;
HttpOnly; SameSite=Strict";
```

4. Avoid Exposing Sensitive Data

Never expose sensitive data (such as API keys, tokens, or passwords) in the front-end code. Always store such data securely on the server side.

Preventing Cross-Site Scripting (XSS) and Cross-Site Request Forgery (CSRF)

1. Preventing XSS (Cross-Site Scripting)

XSS is one of the most common attacks in which an attacker injects malicious scripts into web pages viewed by other users. Vue.js is relatively secure against XSS because it escapes data interpolated into the DOM by default. However, XSS vulnerabilities can still arise when user-generated content is directly injected into the DOM.

Key strategies for preventing XSS:

- **Vue's built-in escaping**: Vue automatically escapes interpolated data (`{{ data }}`) when rendered in the DOM, making it safe from most XSS attacks.

Example:

vue

```
<template>
  <p>{{ userInput }}</p> <!-- Automatically
escaped by Vue -->
</template>
```

However, if you use `v-html`, which allows you to render raw HTML, it opens the door for XSS if you're not careful.

285

Example of potential vulnerability:

```vue
<template>
  <div v-html="userInput"></div> <!-- Risk of XSS -->
</template>
```

To mitigate this, sanitize the HTML using a library like **DOMPurify** before binding it to the DOM.

```javascript
import DOMPurify from 'dompurify';

data() {
  return {
    safeInput:
DOMPurify.sanitize(this.userInput)
  };
}
```

2. Preventing CSRF (Cross-Site Request Forgery)

CSRF is an attack that tricks a victim into submitting a request (e.g., making a transfer or changing settings) on a site where they are authenticated, without their knowledge.

To prevent CSRF:

- **Use anti-CSRF tokens**: Include a CSRF token in each request to ensure that the request is from a legitimate user.
- **SameSite Cookies**: Set the `SameSite` attribute on cookies to `Strict` or `Lax` to prevent them from being sent with cross-site requests.

Example of setting a CSRF token in a Vue.js app:

javascript

```
axios.defaults.headers.common['X-CSRF-Token'] = csrfToken;
```

You would need to retrieve this token from the server (e.g., from a meta tag or API endpoint) and attach it to each request.

Secure API Calls and Authentication

When interacting with APIs in Vue.js, it's crucial to ensure that the API calls are secure and that authentication is handled properly.

1. Securing API Calls

Use HTTPS: Always ensure that your API endpoints are served over HTTPS to prevent sensitive data from being exposed during transmission.

Example:

```
javascript
```

```
axios.get('https://api.example.com/secure-
data')
  .then(response => console.log(response))
  .catch(error => console.error(error));
```

2. Authentication Using JWT

If your application uses JWT for authentication, the token should be securely stored and transmitted:

- **Store JWT tokens** in `localStorage` or `sessionStorage`. However, `localStorage` is vulnerable to XSS, so it's important to sanitize inputs and use other methods like HttpOnly cookies when possible.
- **Include JWT in the `Authorization` header** when making requests to secured endpoints.

Example of sending a JWT token in the `Authorization` header:

```
javascript
```

```
axios.defaults.headers.common['Authorization'] =
`Bearer ${jwtToken}`;
```

3. Refreshing Tokens

In a real-world application, JWT tokens have an expiration time. To avoid users being logged out suddenly, implement **token**

refresh mechanisms where the client can get a new token without requiring the user to log in again.

Example of a token refresh strategy:

- The client makes an API request, and if the token has expired, the server responds with a `401 Unauthorized` status.
- The client then sends a request to the token refresh endpoint to obtain a new JWT token.

Real-World Example: Securing an E-Commerce App

Let's consider a **real-world e-commerce app** where users can log in, browse products, and make purchases. We will secure the app by implementing JWT authentication, protecting sensitive routes, and ensuring that API calls are secure.

1. User Authentication

1. **Login.vue** – The login page where the user submits their credentials:

vue

```
<template>
  <div>
    <h1>Login</h1>
    <form @submit.prevent="handleLogin">
```

```
    <input                    v-model="username"
placeholder="Username" required />
    <input v-model="password" type="password"
placeholder="Password" required />
    <button type="submit">Login</button>
  </form>
</div>
</template>

<script>
import axios from 'axios';
import { mapActions } from 'vuex';

export default {
  data() {
    return {
      username: '',
      password: ''
    };
  },
  methods: {
    ...mapActions(['login']),
    async handleLogin() {
      try {
        const        response       =        await
axios.post('https://api.example.com/login', {
          username: this.username,
          password: this.password
        });
```

```
        // Store the JWT token
        localStorage.setItem('authToken',
response.data.token);
        this.login(response.data.user);
        this.$router.push({ name: 'home' });
      } catch (error) {
        console.error('Login failed:', error);
      }
    }
  }
};
</script>
```

In this example:

- The `handleLogin` method sends the user's credentials to the API.
- On successful login, the JWT token is stored in `localStorage`, and the user is redirected to the home page.

2. Protecting Routes

In `Vue Router`, we use a route guard to protect the routes that require authentication.

```
javascript
```

```
const router = new VueRouter({
  routes: [
    {
      path: '/',
      name: 'home',
      component: Home,
      meta: { requiresAuth: true } // This route
requires authentication
    },
    {
      path: '/login',
      name: 'login',
      component: Login
    }
  ]
});

router.beforeEach((to, from, next) => {
  if          (to.matched.some(record          =>
record.meta.requiresAuth)) {
    const                 token                 =
localStorage.getItem('authToken');
    if (!token) {
      next({ name: 'login' });
    } else {
      next();
    }
  } else {
    next();
```

```
  }
});
```

In this code:

- The `beforeEach` navigation guard checks if the route requires authentication and whether the user is logged in.
- If the user is not authenticated, they are redirected to the login page.

3. Securing API Calls

When making API calls for sensitive data, ensure the JWT token is sent in the `Authorization` header:

```
javascript
```

```
axios.defaults.headers.common['Authorization'] =
`Bearer ${localStorage.getItem('authToken')}`;
```

Summary

In this chapter, we explored several key aspects of securing Vue.js applications:

- **Security best practices** for front-end development, including avoiding inline JavaScript, sanitizing inputs, and using secure cookies.
- Techniques for preventing **XSS** and **CSRF** attacks in Vue.js.

- How to make **secure API calls** using **JWT authentication** and protect routes using Vue Router.
- A **real-world example** of securing an **e-commerce app**, including login, route protection, and securing API interactions.

By following these security practices, you can ensure that your Vue.js application is protected from common vulnerabilities, keeping your users and data safe.

CHAPTER 24

VUE.JS AND REAL-TIME APPLICATIONS

Introduction to Real-Time Web Apps

Real-time web applications allow for instantaneous data exchange between the client and the server. These applications enable users to interact with each other or with data that updates in real-time, without needing to refresh the page or request new data. Common examples of real-time applications include:

- **Chat applications** (e.g., Slack, WhatsApp Web).
- **Live feeds** (e.g., Twitter, Facebook newsfeeds).
- **Collaborative tools** (e.g., Google Docs).
- **Gaming apps** that allow multiple players to interact in real-time.

In this chapter, we will explore how to build real-time applications using Vue.js and WebSockets. Specifically, we will:

1. **Understand the basics of real-time web apps**.
2. **Learn how to use WebSockets** for real-time communication in Vue.js.
3. **Build a real-time chat application** using Vue and Socket.io.

4. A **real-world example** of building a **chat app** with Vue.js and Socket.io.

Using WebSockets with Vue.js

WebSockets provide a full-duplex communication channel that allows for continuous data exchange between the client and the server. Unlike traditional HTTP requests, which require a request-response cycle, WebSockets maintain an open connection, enabling real-time communication.

How WebSockets Work

1. **WebSocket handshake**: The client establishes a WebSocket connection with the server via a special HTTP request (`ws://` or `wss://` for secure connections).
2. **Open connection**: Once the connection is established, both the client and server can send messages back and forth over the same connection.
3. **Close connection**: Either the client or server can close the WebSocket connection when it is no longer needed.

Why WebSockets?

- **Low latency**: WebSockets offer much lower latency compared to traditional HTTP polling.

- **Efficiency**: Since the connection is persistent, there is no need to repeatedly open new connections for every interaction.
- **Scalability**: WebSockets allow you to build real-time apps that scale efficiently for multiple users.

Setting up WebSockets in Vue.js

To integrate WebSockets with Vue.js, we can use libraries like **Socket.io**, which provides an easy-to-use API for real-time bidirectional communication.

1. **Install Socket.io client**:

```bash
bash
```

```bash
npm install socket.io-client
```

2. **Create a WebSocket connection** in a Vue component:

```vue
vue
```

```vue
<template>
  <div>
    <h1>Real-Time Chat</h1>
    <div     v-for="message     in     messages"
:key="message.id">
      <p>{{ message.user }}: {{ message.text
}}</p>
```

```
    </div>
    <input                    v-model="newMessage"
placeholder="Type your message" />
    <button @click="sendMessage">Send</button>
  </div>
</template>

<script>
import io from 'socket.io-client';

export default {
  data() {
    return {
      socket: null,
      messages: [],
      newMessage: ''
    };
  },
  created() {
    // Establish a WebSocket connection to the
server
    this.socket = io('http://localhost:3000');

    // Listen for incoming messages
    this.socket.on('message', (message) => {
      this.messages.push(message);
    });
  },
  methods: {
```

```
    sendMessage() {
      if (this.newMessage.trim()) {
        const message = {
          user: 'User1',
          text: this.newMessage,
          id: Date.now()
        };
        // Send message to the server
        this.socket.emit('sendMessage',
message);
        this.newMessage = '';
      }
    }
  },
  beforeDestroy() {
    // Disconnect from the WebSocket server when
the component is destroyed
    if (this.socket) {
      this.socket.disconnect();
    }
  }
};
</script>
```

In this example:

- **io('http://localhost:3000')** establishes a
  connection to the WebSocket server running at
  localhost:3000.

- **`socket.on('message')`** listens for incoming messages and updates the `messages` array.
- **`socket.emit('sendMessage')`** sends a message to the server.
- The WebSocket connection is cleaned up when the component is destroyed by calling **`socket.disconnect()`**.

Building a Real-Time Chat Application

Let's walk through how to build a **real-time chat application** with Vue.js and **Socket.io**. We will need a back-end server that handles WebSocket connections and broadcasts messages to all connected clients.

1. Set up the Server with Socket.io

To begin, we need to create a Node.js server with Socket.io. This server will listen for incoming WebSocket connections, accept messages from clients, and broadcast messages to all connected clients.

1. **Install dependencies**:

bash

```
npm init -y
npm install express socket.io
```

2. Create a server with Express and Socket.io:

javascript

```javascript
// server.js
const express = require('express');
const http = require('http');
const socketIo = require('socket.io');

const app = express();
const server = http.createServer(app);
const io = socketIo(server);

app.get('/', (req, res) => {
  res.send('WebSocket server is running');
});

// Handle WebSocket connections
io.on('connection', (socket) => {
  console.log('A user connected');

  // Listen for incoming messages
  socket.on('sendMessage', (message) => {
    console.log('Message received:', message);
    // Broadcast message to all connected clients
    io.emit('message', message);
  });

  // Handle disconnect
  socket.on('disconnect', () => {
```

```
    console.log('A user disconnected');
  });
});

// Start the server on port 3000
server.listen(3000, () => {
  console.log('Server      is      running      on
http://localhost:3000');
});
```

This server listens on port 3000 and listens for incoming WebSocket connections using **Socket.io**. When a client sends a message, the server broadcasts it to all other connected clients.

2. Set up the Vue.js Client

We already covered how to set up the **Vue.js client** to send and receive messages. The `socket.on('message')` listener in the Vue component will update the chat interface when new messages arrive.

3. Run the Server and Client

1. Start the Node.js server:

bash

```
node server.js
```

2. Start the Vue.js application:

```bash
```

```
npm run serve
```

Now, open the app in two different browser tabs or windows. You should be able to send messages in one tab, and they will immediately appear in the other tab in real time.

Real-World Example: Building a Chat App with Vue and Socket.io

In a real-world scenario, such as building a **chat application**, you can extend the basic chat app by adding features like:

- **User authentication**: Ensure that users can sign in and receive messages only for their chat room.
- **Private messaging**: Send messages to specific users or groups.
- **Message persistence**: Store messages in a database and retrieve them when a user reconnects.
- **Typing indicators**: Show when other users are typing.

Adding Typing Indicators

Let's add a typing indicator to the chat app to notify other users when someone is typing a message.

1. **Update the Vue component** to emit a `typing` event when the user starts typing:

vue

```
<template>
  <div>
    <h1>Real-Time Chat</h1>
    <div     v-for="message     in     messages"
:key="message.id">
      <p>{{ message.user }}: {{ message.text
}}</p>
    </div>
    <input
      v-model="newMessage"
      placeholder="Type your message"
      @input="onTyping"
    />
    <p v-if="isTyping">Someone is typing...</p>
    <button @click="sendMessage">Send</button>
  </div>
</template>

<script>
export default {
  data() {
    return {
      socket: null,
      messages: [],
```

```
    newMessage: '',
    isTyping: false
  };
},
created() {
  this.socket = io('http://localhost:3000');
  this.socket.on('message', (message) => {
    this.messages.push(message);
  });
  this.socket.on('typing', () => {
    this.isTyping = true;
    setTimeout(() => {
      this.isTyping = false;
    }, 3000);
  });
},
methods: {
  sendMessage() {
    if (this.newMessage.trim()) {
      const message = {
        user: 'User1',
        text: this.newMessage,
        id: Date.now()
      };
      this.socket.emit('sendMessage',
message);
      this.newMessage = '';
    }
  },
```

```
  onTyping() {
    this.socket.emit('typing');
  }
},
beforeDestroy() {
  if (this.socket) {
    this.socket.disconnect();
  }
}
};
</script>
```

2. **Update the server** to broadcast the typing event:

```javascript
io.on('connection', (socket) => {
  console.log('A user connected');

  socket.on('sendMessage', (message) => {
    io.emit('message', message);
  });

  socket.on('typing', () => {
    socket.broadcast.emit('typing');
  });

  socket.on('disconnect', () => {
    console.log('A user disconnected');
  });
```

306

```
});
```

In this updated version of the app:

- The client emits a `typing` event when the user starts typing, and the server broadcasts the `typing` event to other clients.
- When another user is typing, the `isTyping` flag is set to `true` and a "Someone is typing..." message is displayed.

Summary

In this chapter, we explored how to build **real-time applications** in Vue.js using **WebSockets** and **Socket.io**:

- **WebSockets** allow bidirectional, low-latency communication, making them ideal for real-time applications.
- We built a **real-time chat app** with Vue.js and Socket.io, enabling instant message exchanges between clients.
- We also added features such as **typing indicators** to enhance the user experience.

Real-time applications are an essential part of modern web development, and with Vue.js and WebSockets, building these apps has never been easier. In the next chapter, we will explore how to integrate Vue.js with back-end services to handle complex real-time data and improve the scalability of real-time features.

CHAPTER 25

SERVER-SIDE RENDERING WITH VUE.JS

Introduction

Server-Side Rendering (SSR) is a technique used to render the content of a web page on the server rather than in the browser. With SSR, the server generates the complete HTML of a page before sending it to the browser, which improves performance, search engine optimization (SEO), and the initial loading experience for users.

In this chapter, we will explore:

1. What **Server-Side Rendering (SSR)** is and why it is important.
2. The **benefits of SSR** in Vue.js applications.
3. How to use **Nuxt.js**, a framework built on top of Vue.js that simplifies SSR.
4. A **real-world example** of building a **blog** with SSR using Nuxt.js.

By the end of this chapter, you'll understand how to integrate SSR into your Vue.js applications and the advantages it offers for both performance and SEO.

What is Server-Side Rendering (SSR)?

In traditional client-side rendering (CSR), the browser loads a JavaScript file and then dynamically generates the HTML content on the client side. However, in SSR, the HTML is rendered on the server, and the fully rendered page is sent to the client. This process allows the browser to display the page more quickly and improves the user experience, especially on slower networks or devices.

How SSR Works:

1. **Initial Request**: The browser sends an HTTP request to the server for a specific page.
2. **Server Processing**: The server renders the requested page, which may involve fetching data and rendering it into an HTML template.
3. **HTML Response**: The server sends back the fully rendered HTML page to the client.
4. **Hydration**: Once the HTML is loaded on the client side, Vue.js takes over, attaching event listeners and enabling interactivity. This process is called "hydration."

SSR is particularly useful for websites with content that needs to be indexed by search engines (e.g., blogs, e-commerce sites) or when you want to provide a faster initial loading experience.

Benefits of SSR in Vue.js

SSR brings several key advantages to Vue.js applications:

1. Improved Performance (Faster Initial Load)

SSR sends a fully rendered HTML page to the client, allowing the browser to display the content quickly. This is especially important for users with slower network connections or devices, as they can view the page without waiting for the entire JavaScript bundle to load and execute.

2. Better SEO (Search Engine Optimization)

With SSR, search engine crawlers can crawl the fully rendered HTML page instead of having to rely on JavaScript execution to render the content. This makes it easier for search engines to index the content, which improves the app's SEO performance.

For single-page applications (SPAs) that rely on CSR, search engines might struggle to index content dynamically loaded by JavaScript. With SSR, the content is immediately available in the initial HTML response, improving indexing and visibility.

3. Enhanced Social Media Sharing

When sharing content on social media platforms (e.g., Facebook, Twitter), they often scrape the page's metadata (e.g., title,

310

description, image). With SSR, this metadata is available in the initial HTML response, making it easier for platforms to extract the correct data.

4. Improved User Experience

With SSR, the user can see the page content faster because the HTML is already rendered by the server. This results in a more fluid and responsive experience, particularly for first-time users or slow network conditions.

Introduction to Nuxt.js for SSR

While Vue.js is a powerful framework for building client-side applications, setting up SSR manually can be complex and time-consuming. **Nuxt.js** is a framework built on top of Vue.js that simplifies the process of setting up SSR for your Vue applications.

Nuxt.js provides:

- **Automatic SSR setup**: Nuxt automatically handles SSR, so you don't need to configure it manually.
- **Vue Router integration**: Nuxt uses Vue Router and provides a file-based routing system that simplifies navigation and page structure.
- **Automatic code splitting**: Nuxt automatically splits your code into smaller bundles, improving performance by only loading the necessary parts of the app.

- **Static site generation (SSG)**: Nuxt also supports generating static sites, where the app is pre-rendered at build time and can be deployed as static HTML files.

Nuxt.js makes SSR easy to implement, even for large-scale applications. It also offers the flexibility to choose between SSR, CSR, and static site generation, depending on your needs.

Setting Up a Nuxt.js Project

To get started with Nuxt.js, we need to create a new Nuxt project. The following steps will guide you through setting up Nuxt.js for SSR.

1. Install Nuxt.js

First, install **Nuxt.js** by running the following commands:

bash

```
npx create-nuxt-app my-blog
```

This command will create a new Nuxt.js project in the `my-blog` directory. During the setup, you'll be prompted to choose some options such as:

- Package manager (npm or yarn)
- UI framework (e.g., Vuetify, Tailwind CSS, or none)
- Linting tools

312

- Testing frameworks

2. Run the Nuxt.js Development Server

After the setup is complete, navigate to the project folder and run the development server:

```bash
cd my-blog
npm run dev
```

This will start the Nuxt.js app in development mode at `http://localhost:3000`. You can now begin developing your SSR-enabled Vue.js application.

Real-World Example: Building a Blog with SSR

Let's build a simple **blog application** using Nuxt.js with SSR. The blog will have a home page that lists posts and a detail page for individual posts.

1. Create Pages for the Blog

Nuxt.js uses a file-based routing system. The pages are automatically created based on the files you put in the `pages` directory.

- **Home.vue** (Listing Blog Posts):

Create a file `pages/index.vue` to display the list of blog posts.

vue

```vue
<template>
  <div>
    <h1>Blog Posts</h1>
    <ul>
      <li v-for="post in posts" :key="post.id">
        <nuxt-link :to="'/post/' + post.id">{{
post.title }}</nuxt-link>
      </li>
    </ul>
  </div>
</template>

<script>
export default {
  async asyncData() {
    // Fetch the blog posts from an API or a
static file
    const                res                =                await
fetch('https://jsonplaceholder.typicode.com/pos
ts');
    const posts = await res.json();
    return { posts };
  }
};
</script>
```

In this example:

- The `asyncData` method is used to fetch data before the page is rendered, enabling SSR.
- The blog posts are fetched from an external API (`jsonplaceholder.typicode.com` in this case).
- **PostDetail.vue** (Viewing a Single Post):

Create a file `pages/post/_id.vue` to display the details of a single blog post.

vue

```vue
<template>
  <div>
    <h1>{{ post.title }}</h1>
    <p>{{ post.body }}</p>
  </div>
</template>

<script>
export default {
  async asyncData({ params }) {
    // Fetch the specific post based on the ID
from the URL
    const           res        =          await
fetch(`https://jsonplaceholder.typicode.com/pos
ts/${params.id}`);
    const post = await res.json();
```

```
    return { post };
  }
};
</script>
```

In this example:

- We use Nuxt's dynamic routing (_id.vue) to fetch and display a single post based on the URL parameter (params.id).
- asyncData ensures that the post data is fetched server-side before rendering the page.

2. Add Some Basic Styling

You can add CSS to your app by creating a assets/css folder and adding a global stylesheet (global.css):

css

```css
/* assets/css/global.css */
body {
  font-family: Arial, sans-serif;
  line-height: 1.6;
}

h1 {
  color: #42b983;
}
```

Then, in `nuxt.config.js`, import the CSS file:

javascript

```javascript
// nuxt.config.js
export default {
  css: ['@/assets/css/global.css']
};
```

3. Build and Deploy

Once your app is ready, you can build it for production. Run the following command to generate the production build:

bash

```bash
npm run build
```

To start the SSR app in production mode, run:

bash

```bash
npm run start
```

This will launch the app in server-side rendering mode, and the pages will be pre-rendered on the server before being sent to the client.

For deployment, you can deploy the app to any platform that supports Node.js (e.g., **Heroku**, **Netlify**, **Vercel**).

317

Summary

In this chapter, we learned about **Server-Side Rendering (SSR)** and how it improves performance and SEO for Vue.js applications. We covered:

- What SSR is and how it differs from traditional client-side rendering.
- The **benefits of SSR** in Vue.js, including faster initial load times, better SEO, and improved user experience.
- **Nuxt.js**, a framework built on top of Vue.js that simplifies the process of building SSR applications.
- A **real-world example** of building a **blog** using SSR with Nuxt.js, including routing, fetching data, and deploying the app.

By using Nuxt.js, we can easily set up SSR for Vue.js apps and take advantage of features like code splitting, automatic routing, and static site generation. With SSR, your Vue.js apps will be faster, more SEO-friendly, and ready to handle a larger audience.

CHAPTER 26

VUE 3 AND THE COMPOSITION API

Introduction to Vue 3 and Composition API

Vue 3 introduces a major update to the Vue.js framework, including new features that improve the developer experience and application performance. One of the most significant changes in Vue 3 is the **Composition API**, a new way to organize and write Vue components. It provides a more flexible and reusable approach to working with reactive data, computed properties, and lifecycle hooks.

Before Vue 3, Vue developers primarily used the **Options API**, which organizes code based on component options (e.g., `data`, `methods`, `computed`, `watch`). While the Options API is still fully supported in Vue 3, the Composition API allows developers to group related logic together, making the code more maintainable and scalable, especially in larger applications.

In this chapter, we will cover:

1. **Introduction to Vue 3** and the **Composition API**.
2. **Benefits of using the Composition API** in your Vue 3 applications.

319

3. How to **refactor existing Vue 2 components** using the Options API to use the Composition API.

4. A **real-world example** of converting a **Vue 2 app to Vue 3** using the Composition API.

By the end of this chapter, you will understand how to adopt the Composition API in your Vue 3 projects and how it improves the flexibility and reusability of your components.

What is the Composition API?

The Composition API is a new way to write Vue components introduced in Vue 3. It provides a more function-based approach to organizing component logic, as opposed to the Options API, which is more declarative. With the Composition API, developers can group related logic together in functions, making it easier to compose and reuse functionality.

Basic Syntax of the Composition API

- **ref**: A function that creates a reactive reference to a value.
- **reactive**: A function that makes an object reactive.
- **computed**: A function that creates a computed property.
- **watch**: A function that watches for changes to a reactive value.

- **onMounted**, **onUnmounted**, and other lifecycle hooks: Functions that correspond to Vue component lifecycle events.

In the Composition API, component logic is typically grouped inside the setup() function, which is called when the component is created. Inside setup(), you can use ref, reactive, computed, and other Composition API functions to manage your component's state and behavior.

```javascript
// Example of the Composition API
import { ref, computed, onMounted } from 'vue';

export default {
  setup() {
    const count = ref(0);

    const doubleCount = computed(() => count.value * 2);

    onMounted(() => {
      console.log('Component is mounted');
    });

    return {
      count,
      doubleCount
```

```
    };
  }
};
```

In this example:

- **count** is a reactive reference using the `ref` function.
- **doubleCount** is a computed property.
- **onMounted** logs a message when the component is mounted.

Benefits of Using the Composition API

The Composition API offers several advantages over the Options API, especially for larger applications:

1. Better Code Organization

With the Composition API, you can group related logic together in a more modular and reusable way. In the Options API, logic is organized into separate options (`data`, `methods`, `computed`, etc.), which can become scattered and harder to manage as components grow in size. The Composition API allows you to organize logic by feature, which can make your components more readable and maintainable.

Example:

- **Options API**: Component logic is scattered into `data`, `methods`, `computed`, and `watch` sections.
- **Composition API**: Related logic is grouped together inside the `setup()` function.

2. Improved Reusability

The Composition API allows for better code reuse. You can extract reactive state and logic into reusable functions (called **composables**). This is especially useful when you need to share logic across multiple components without duplicating code.

Example:

```javascript
// useCounter.js (Composable function)
import { ref } from 'vue';

export function useCounter() {
  const count = ref(0);

  const increment = () => {
    count.value++;
  };

  return {
    count,
    increment
```

```
    };
}
```

You can then use this `useCounter` composable in any component:

```javascript
import { useCounter } from './useCounter';

export default {
  setup() {
    const { count, increment } = useCounter();
    return { count, increment };
  }
};
```

3. Better TypeScript Support

Vue 3's Composition API is more TypeScript-friendly. The setup function allows for better type inference, making it easier to work with TypeScript in your Vue components.

4. More Flexible Composition

The Composition API provides more flexibility when it comes to structuring components. It allows you to dynamically add reactive data, computed properties, and methods, providing more control over the component's logic.

324

Refactoring Options API to Composition API

If you're upgrading an existing Vue 2 app to Vue 3 or just want to refactor a component from the Options API to the Composition API, the process involves moving logic from the `data`, `methods`, `computed`, and `watch` options into the `setup()` function.

1. Refactoring `data` to `ref` or `reactive`

In the Options API, `data` is used to define reactive state:

javascript

```
// Options API
export default {
  data() {
    return {
      count: 0
    };
  }
};
```

In the Composition API, you use `ref` for primitive values and `reactive` for objects:

javascript

```
// Composition API
import { ref } from 'vue';
```

```javascript
export default {
  setup() {
    const count = ref(0);
    return { count };
  }
};
```

2. Refactoring methods to functions inside setup

In the Options API, methods are defined inside the methods option:

javascript

```javascript
// Options API
export default {
  methods: {
    increment() {
      this.count++;
    }
  }
};
```

In the Composition API, methods are defined as functions inside setup():

javascript

```javascript
// Composition API
```

```
export default {
  setup() {
    const count = ref(0);
    const increment = () => {
      count.value++;
    };
    return { count, increment };
  }
};
```

3. Refactoring computed to computed in the Composition API

In the Options API, computed properties are defined inside the computed option:

javascript

```
// Options API
export default {
  computed: {
    doubleCount() {
      return this.count * 2;
    }
  }
};
```

In the Composition API, computed properties are created using the computed function:

javascript

```
// Composition API
import { computed } from 'vue';

export default {
  setup() {
    const count = ref(0);
    const   doubleCount   =   computed(()   =>
count.value * 2);
    return { count, doubleCount };
  }
};
```

4. Refactoring watch to watch in the Composition API

In the Options API, watch is defined inside the watch option:

```
javascript
```

```
// Options API
export default {
  watch: {
    count(newCount) {
      console.log('Count changed to', newCount);
    }
  }
};
```

In the Composition API, watch is used as a function inside setup():

328

```javascript

// Composition API
import { watch } from 'vue';

export default {
  setup() {
    const count = ref(0);
    watch(count, (newCount) => {
      console.log('Count changed to', newCount);
    });
    return { count };
  }
};
```

Real-World Example: Converting a Vue 2 App to Vue 3

Let's convert a basic Vue 2 app (built using the Options API) to Vue 3 using the Composition API.

1. Vue 2 App Using Options API

Here is a simple Vue 2 app using the Options API:

```javascript

// Vue 2 App
new Vue({
  el: '#app',
  data() {
```

```
    return {
      message: 'Hello, Vue 2!',
      count: 0
    };
  },
  methods: {
    increment() {
      this.count++;
    }
  },
  computed: {
    doubleCount() {
      return this.count * 2;
    }
  }
});
```

2. Refactored Vue 3 App Using Composition API

We can refactor the above app to Vue 3 using the Composition API:

javascript

```
// Vue 3 App with Composition API
import { createApp, ref, computed } from 'vue';

const App = {
  setup() {
    const message = ref('Hello, Vue 3!');
```

```
const count = ref(0);

const increment = () => {
  count.value++;
};

const doubleCount = computed(() =>
count.value * 2);

  return {
    message,
    count,
    increment,
    doubleCount
  };
}
};

createApp(App).mount('#app');
```

In this refactor:

- `data` is replaced with `ref`.
- `methods` are replaced with regular functions.
- `computed` is used to create computed properties inside `setup()`.

3. Benefits of Refactoring

- **Better organization**: Grouping related logic together makes the code easier to maintain, especially as the app grows.

- **Improved reusability**: We can extract common functionality into **composables**, which can be reused across multiple components.

- **TypeScript support**: The Composition API works seamlessly with TypeScript, making type inference and declaration easier.

Summary

In this chapter, we explored the **Composition API** in Vue 3 and how it improves the way we structure and organize components:

- **Vue 3 Composition API** provides a flexible, function-based approach to manage reactive data, computed properties, and lifecycle hooks.

- We discussed the **benefits** of using the Composition API, such as better code organization, improved reusability, and better TypeScript support.

- We learned how to **refactor Vue 2 components** from the Options API to the Composition API.

- A **real-world example** was provided for converting a basic Vue 2 app to Vue 3 using the Composition API.

By adopting the Composition API, you can write more maintainable, flexible, and scalable Vue applications, especially as your app grows in complexity.

CHAPTER 27

ADVANCED TOPICS IN VUE.JS

Introduction

Vue.js is a powerful and flexible framework for building modern web applications. As you become more experienced with Vue, you may need to dive into more **advanced topics** to tackle complex applications. In this chapter, we will cover:

1. **Custom Directives** and **Mixins** for extending Vue's functionality.
2. **Advanced state management patterns** using Vuex.
3. Using **TypeScript** with Vue.js to enhance type safety and development experience.
4. A **real-world example** of building a **complex dashboard app** using Vue.js, incorporating the concepts discussed.

By the end of this chapter, you will have the skills to implement advanced features in your Vue.js applications and improve code maintainability and scalability.

Custom Directives and Mixins

Vue.js allows developers to extend the framework's functionality by creating **custom directives** and **mixins**. These tools allow you to reuse logic and add special behavior to elements or components in a more modular way.

1. Custom Directives

Vue provides built-in directives like `v-if`, `v-for`, `v-bind`, and `v-model`. However, you can also create your own **custom directives** when you need to add custom behavior to DOM elements.

For example, let's create a custom directive to automatically focus an element when it is inserted into the DOM.

Creating a Custom Directive: `v-focus`

To create a custom directive, you use the `Vue.directive` method, where you define the directive's name and its lifecycle hooks.

javascript

```
// main.js
Vue.directive('focus', {
  inserted(el) {
    el.focus();
```

```
  }
});
```

You can now use the `v-focus` directive on any element to automatically focus it when the component is rendered:

vue

```
<template>
  <div>
    <input v-focus placeholder="This will be
focused when the page loads" />
  </div>
</template>
```

This example shows how you can create a directive to add custom behavior to a DOM element in a reusable way.

2. Mixins

Mixins are a way to share reusable logic between components. You can use mixins to add functionality like data, methods, lifecycle hooks, and computed properties that can be reused across different components.

Creating a Mixin

Here's an example of a mixin that contains common data and methods for tracking user login state:

336

javascript

```javascript
// authMixin.js
export const authMixin = {
  data() {
    return {
      isAuthenticated: false,
      username: ''
    };
  },
  methods: {
    login(user) {
      this.isAuthenticated = true;
      this.username = user.username;
    },
    logout() {
      this.isAuthenticated = false;
      this.username = '';
    }
  }
};
```

Now, you can import and use the `authMixin` in any Vue component:

vue

```vue
<template>
  <div>
```

```
    <p     v-if="isAuthenticated">Welcome,     {{
username }}</p>
    <p v-else>Please log in.</p>
    <button @click="login({ username: 'JohnDoe'
})">Log in</button>
    <button @click="logout">Log out</button>
  </div>
</template>

<script>
import { authMixin } from './authMixin';

export default {
  mixins: [authMixin]
};
</script>
```

By using mixins, we avoid repeating the login/logout logic across multiple components, making the code more maintainable and DRY (Don't Repeat Yourself).

Advanced State Management Patterns

Managing state efficiently is key to building scalable applications. Vuex is Vue's official state management library, but as the complexity of the application grows, it may require more advanced state management patterns.

1. Vuex Modules

In Vuex, you can split the store into **modules**. Each module has its own state, mutations, actions, and getters, which makes it easier to manage state in large applications.

javascript

```javascript
// store/modules/auth.js
export const auth = {
  state: {
    isAuthenticated: false,
    username: ''
  },
  mutations: {
    login(state, username) {
      state.isAuthenticated = true;
      state.username = username;
    },
    logout(state) {
      state.isAuthenticated = false;
      state.username = '';
    }
  },
  actions: {
    login({ commit }, username) {
      commit('login', username);
    },
    logout({ commit }) {
```

```
      commit('logout');
    }
  },
  getters: {
    isAuthenticated:            state            =>
state.isAuthenticated,
    username: state => state.username
  }
};
```

Now you can combine the modules in the main Vuex store:

```javascript

import Vue from 'vue';
import Vuex from 'vuex';
import { auth } from './modules/auth';

Vue.use(Vuex);

export default new Vuex.Store({
  modules: {
    auth
  }
});
```

2. Using Actions for Asynchronous Operations

In larger applications, you often need to perform asynchronous operations, such as API calls. You can use Vuex **actions** for handling these operations.

Example: Fetching data asynchronously in Vuex:

```javascript
// store/modules/posts.js
export const posts = {
  state: {
    posts: []
  },
  mutations: {
    setPosts(state, posts) {
      state.posts = posts;
    }
  },
  actions: {
    async fetchPosts({ commit }) {
      const response = await fetch('https://jsonplaceholder.typicode.com/posts');
      const posts = await response.json();
      commit('setPosts', posts);
    }
  },
```

```
getters: {
  allPosts: state => state.posts
}
};
```

You can then dispatch the `fetchPosts` action from a component:

vue

```
<template>
  <div>
    <ul>
      <li     v-for="post     in     posts"
:key="post.id">{{ post.title }}</li>
    </ul>
  </div>
</template>

<script>
export default {
  computed: {
    posts() {
      return
this.$store.getters['posts/allPosts'];
    }
  },
  created() {
    this.$store.dispatch('posts/fetchPosts');
  }
};
```

```
</script>
```

This ensures that all asynchronous operations (such as fetching data) are handled in Vuex, keeping your components cleaner and more focused on presentation logic.

TypeScript with Vue.js

Vue 3 provides better **TypeScript** support than Vue 2, allowing developers to write safer and more maintainable code with static typing.

Setting Up TypeScript in Vue 3

To use TypeScript in Vue 3, you need to:

1. Install TypeScript and the Vue 3 TypeScript loader:

```bash
```

```
npm    install    typescript    @vue/cli-plugin-
typescript --save-dev
```

2. Configure the project to use TypeScript by creating a `tsconfig.json` file and adding type definitions for Vue.

Example of a `tsconfig.json`:

343

json

```json
{
  "compilerOptions": {
    "target": "es5",
    "lib": ["dom", "es2015"],
    "module": "esnext",
    "moduleResolution": "node",
    "jsx": "preserve",
    "esModuleInterop": true,
    "strict": true,
    "skipLibCheck": true,
    "forceConsistentCasingInFileNames": true,
    "resolveJsonModule": true
  },
  "include": [
    "src/**/*.ts",
    "src/**/*.d.ts",
    "src/**/*.tsx",
    "src/**/*.vue"
  ]
}
```

Now, you can use TypeScript in your `.vue` files. For example:

vue

```vue
<template>
  <div>{{ message }}</div>
</template>
```

```
<script lang="ts">
export default {
  data() {
    return {
      message: 'Hello, TypeScript in Vue!'
    };
  }
};
</script>
```

Vue 3 uses `lang="ts"` in the `<script>` tag to enable TypeScript support in your `.vue` components.

Using Types in Vue Components

TypeScript allows you to define types for your component's props, data, and methods. Here's an example of a component with TypeScript:

vue

```
<template>
  <div>{{ count }}</div>
</template>

<script lang="ts">
import { defineComponent, ref } from 'vue';
```

```
export default defineComponent({
  name: 'Counter',
  setup() {
    const count = ref<number>(0);

    const increment = () => {
      count.value++;
    };

    return { count, increment };
  }
});
</script>
```

In this example, we define the type of the `count` variable as `number`, ensuring type safety in the component.

Real-World Example: Building a Complex Dashboard App

Now, let's put all the concepts together and build a **complex dashboard app** that leverages Vue 3 features like the Composition API, Vuex for state management, TypeScript for type safety, and custom components.

1. Project Setup

Start by setting up the project with Vue 3 and TypeScript:

```bash
bash
```

```bash
vue create dashboard-app
```

Select **Vue 3** and **TypeScript** during setup.

2. Creating the Dashboard Layout

Create a main `Dashboard.vue` component with a navigation sidebar and content area.

```vue
vue
```

```vue
<template>
  <div class="dashboard">
    <Sidebar />
    <div class="content">
      <h1>Dashboard</h1>
      <DataDisplay />
    </div>
  </div>
</template>

<script lang="ts">
import Sidebar from './Sidebar.vue';
import DataDisplay from './DataDisplay.vue';

export default {
  components: {
    Sidebar,
```

```
      DataDisplay
  }
};
</script>
```

3. State Management with Vuex

Set up a Vuex store to manage the state of the dashboard, such as user data and statistics:

```typescript
// store/modules/user.ts
import { Module } from 'vuex';

interface UserState {
  name: string;
  loggedIn: boolean;
}

const user: Module<UserState, any> = {
  state: {
    name: 'John Doe',
    loggedIn: false
  },
  mutations: {
    logIn(state) {
      state.loggedIn = true;
    },
    logOut(state) {
```

```
    state.loggedIn = false;
  }
 }
};
```

```
export default user;
```

4. Using TypeScript for Component Logic

With TypeScript, we ensure that our component properties are properly typed and help with better autocompletion and error-checking.

vue

```
<script lang="ts">
import { defineComponent, ref } from 'vue';

export default defineComponent({
  setup() {
    const count = ref<number>(0);
    const increment = () => count.value++;

    return { count, increment };
  }
});
</script>
```

5. Deploying the App

Once your dashboard app is ready, build it for production using:

```bash
bash
```

```bash
npm run build
```

Then, deploy it to a service like **Netlify**, **Heroku**, or any platform that supports Node.js apps.

Summary

In this chapter, we covered advanced topics in Vue.js:

- **Custom Directives** and **Mixins** to extend functionality and reuse code.
- **Advanced state management patterns** using Vuex modules and asynchronous actions.
- The integration of **TypeScript** in Vue 3 for better type safety and a smoother development experience.
- A **real-world example** of building a **complex dashboard app** using the Composition API, Vuex, and TypeScript.

By mastering these advanced features, you can build scalable, maintainable, and highly performant Vue.js applications.